RUSTIC

French

Cooking

MADE EASY

RUSTIC *French* *Cooking* MADE EASY

Authentic, Regional Flavors from
Provence, Brittany, Alsace and Beyond

AUDREY LE GOFF

Creator of Pardon Your French

PAGE STREET
PUBLISHING CO.

PAGE STREET
PUBLISHING CO.

First published in 2019 by
Page Street Publishing Co.
27 Congress Street, Suite 105
Salem, MA 01970
www.pagestreetpublishing.com

Distributed by Macmillan, sales in Canada by The Canadian Manda Group.

23   22   21   20   19   1   2   3   4   5

ISBN-13: 978-1-62414-863-7
ISBN-10: 1-62414-863-8

Library of Congress Control Number: 2019932131

Cover and book design by Rosie Stewart for Page Street Publishing Co.

Photography by Audrey Le Goff and Karly Schaefer

Printed and bound in China

Dedication

To my beloved France.

Contents

DESSERTS MAISON // HOMEY DESSERTS — 107

LE GOÛTER // AFTERNOON TREATS — 145

Introduction

I was born and raised in Brittany, on the northwestern Atlantic coast of France. My favorite meals were—and well, still are—buckwheat crêpes filled with andouillette (tripe sausage) with a glass of fermented milk, pungent fish soup with crusty croutons, fresh periwinkles on rye bread with salted butter, craggy apple flans and butter-oozing Kouign-Amanns (page 114). In other words, a far stretch from what French cuisine is usually known for, outside of France.

As a child, I was lucky enough to travel throughout France with my family. We spent cold December holidays in eastern Alsace, eating billowy yeasted cakes (Kugelhopf, page 141). In February, we would often go to the snowy Jura mountains or the French Alps, and enjoy our breakfast toasts with Alpine honey and chestnut spread. We visited Basque Country on the Spanish border, where I was introduced to fiery dishes sprinkled with Espelette pepper. We visited Burgundy, where I bit into my first baked cheese puffs (page 21). The ducks of Dordogne, the sausages of Toulouse, the sweet lemons of Corsica, the creamy cheeses of Normandy . . . we did that too.

For university, I moved to Rennes in central Brittany, where my love for buckwheat crêpes and buttery treats only grew stronger. I then moved to Lyon, often considered the world's food capital, where I found a whole new world of fine delicatessen meats, cheese spreads (page 25) and nut-centric desserts. Later on, I fell in love with Provence and its generous, Mediterranean cuisine. And not so long ago, I discovered the Hauts-de-France at the northern tip of the country, with its heart-warming Flemish beer-infused dishes and sugary treats.

So, as I settled in Canada ten years ago, you can imagine my surprise to see how French cuisine was mostly defined by croissants, only a few sophisticated recipes and a strict and unapproachable cooking style. I realized the canon of French cuisine was in fact as much admired in the rest of the world as it was intimidating. What a contrast from the jolly and unfussy French cuisine I grew up with, the one that had shaped my life.

Since then, I have had an itch to show the world how simple, humble and incredibly diverse French cuisine really is—from a simple French home cook like me, from my little piece of the French countryside.

I wrote this book to show you regional French cuisine, with its rich history and varied ingredients, is tremendously exciting and anything but uniform. I wanted to share a collection of recipes that are authentic and accessible to any home cook, wherever you are in the world. To me, and to many other French people, the heart of French cooking is in home kitchens, and not in fancy restaurants.

This book is a love letter to France, to my passion and appetite for it; to France's regions that are so diverse yet bound by the same love for good food and hospitality; to all these wonderful recipes that deserve to be known, shared and passed on.

Enjoy, and Bon Appétit!

Audrey

L'apéro

Small Bites

L'apéro—short for l'apéritif, or what's known as the French evening prayer— is a pre-meal ritual involving a few drinks and some finger foods. It is a most cherished interlude in the day's activities—a moment of conviviality, which is so dear to the French. You might think of it as happy hour, but for the French, it is a sacred and a quintessential part of social culture. Taking part in this evening ritual perpetuates a feeling of belonging. The food and drink is an added bonus.

While Americans are aficionados of mixed cocktails, the French would rather reach for their locally-produced spirits and liqueurs, which French regions are rich with. But, I feel the real pleasure of it all exists in the delicacies each regional table provides. In Lyon, while in university, I discovered the pleasures of Cervelle de Canut (Herbed Cheese Spread, page 25) while sipping on Beaujolais Nouveau. If you're visiting the chic French Riviera, you'll likely get served squares of a famous Pissaladière (Onion, Anchovy and Black Olive Tart, page 22) or a bowl of Barbajuans (Fried Ravioli, page 26). And whenever I'm visiting Marseille, Panisses (Chickpea Flour Fries, page 14) and a glass of rosé wine are my go-to.

Simplicity and lack of fuss are always prevalent—the simpler the better. An apéro is all about whetting the appetite and getting the conversation flowing . . . .

Préfou

Parsley Butter Garlic Bread

Breads with all sorts of garnishes are a star of the French apéro and this Préfou, a specialty from Vendée in west-central France, is undeniably one of my favorites. It is a succulent ode to simplicity, a humble bread garnished with a flavor-packed garlic and parsley compound butter.

It's said Vendée bakers used to test the heat of their ovens by throwing a handful of dough inside and watching it bake. The barely baked buns would then be eaten with a slab of parsley butter, giving birth to this local specialty. You can now find premade préfous in most grocery stores and bakeries in Vendée, and it is amazingly simple to make at home as well.

When buying the baguette for this recipe, I choose one that is slightly under-baked as it will crisp up and brown in the oven for an additional fifteen minutes.

SERVES 6 TO 8

1 cup (225 g) unsalted butter, at room temperature

1 bunch of flat-leaf parsley, stemmed and finely chopped

4 cloves garlic, peeled, desprouted and minced

½ tsp salt

½ tsp fresh ground black pepper

1 baguette

Preheat your oven to 350°F (180°C, or gas mark 4), with a rack in the middle.

In a bowl, using a fork or a rubber spatula, cream together the butter, parsley, garlic, salt and ground pepper.

Lay the baguette on a parchment-lined baking sheet.

With a serrated bread knife, cut 1-inch (2.5-cm)-thick slices all along the baguette, making sure not to cut through the bread all the way. Generously spread parsley butter in between each cut.

Bake for 15 minutes. Serve immediately, tearing each slice to separate.

Panisses

Chickpea Flour Fries

In Marseille, people don't normally nosh on potato chips before dinner. Instead they enjoy crispy Chickpea Flour Fries called panisses. Chickpea flour mixed with water is the base of this Provençal street food. In Nice—where it is called Socca—and in Toulon—where it is called Cade—this simple mixture is spread thin like a galette and baked in a wood-fire oven. In Marseille, it is cut into circles or sticks and panfried right before serving. Crisp on the outside, creamy on the inside, panisses are often enjoyed on their own with a sprinkle of salt, pepper or dried herbs.

For a complete Provençal experience, eat alongside a glass of pastis (anise-flavored spirit) or with a chilled rosé wine.

SERVES 4 / MAKES 18 TO 20 PANISSES

1⅔ cups (150 g) chickpea flour (see tip)

½ tsp salt

1 tsp baking soda

1¼ cups (300 ml) cold water

Extra-virgin olive oil, for greasing the pan and frying

Salt, fresh ground black pepper and/or dried herbs

In a large bowl, mix together the chickpea flour, salt and baking soda. Slowly pour in the cold water, and whisk until you reach the consistency of a thin pancake batter. If the batter is lumpy, you can use a blender or hand mixer to smooth it out.

Transfer the batter to a medium saucepan. Over medium-low heat, warm up the batter and whisk continuously until the batter begins to clump and get stuck in the whisk. Switch to a wooden spoon or rubber spatula, and mix continuously again for 2 to 3 minutes until the batter thickens. It should reach the consistency of very thick custard that leaves the edges of the saucepan clean.

Transfer the mixture into a well-greased, 8½ x 4½–inch (21.6 x 11.4–cm) loaf pan. Pack it in well, making sure there are no bubbles underneath, and smooth out the surface. Cover the pan with plastic wrap, and place in the fridge for 12 hours or overnight.

Flip the pan and carefully remove the chickpea flour loaf. Dip a large knife into cold water, and slice the loaf into ½-inch (1.3-cm)-thick sticks, just like large potato fries.

Line a large plate with paper towels.

Heat 2 tablespoons (30 ml) of extra-virgin olive oil in a nonstick pan or skillet. In several batches, fry the panisse sticks 2 to 3 minutes on each side until crisp and golden. Transfer the sticks immediately to the paper towel–lined plate to absorb the excess oil. Sprinkle with salt, ground pepper and/or dried herbs to taste. Serve immediately.

FRENCH PANTRY TIP: *Chickpea flour is easy to work with, naturally gluten-free and a must to re-create the street food staples of Provence: Panisses, Socca and Cade. I always keep a bag of it to create quick appetizers. Find it in most natural food stores.*

Fougasse aux Olives Noires et aux Tomates Séchées

Black Olive and Sun-Dried Tomato Fougasse

A hybrid between a pizza dough and the Italian focaccia, the French fougasse is a famous Provençal bread raved about for its soft crust, dense springy crumb and its myriad of varieties. It is one of the great French market staples—in Provence and all over the country. I always keep my eyes open for it when visiting my local market in Brittany.

Making a fougasse at home is an ever-exciting process since you can play with so many variations. Black olive and sun-dried tomato is one of my favorites as it packs a scrumptious salty punch—but feel free to experiment on your own.

A fougasse is perfect for apéro, cut into small pieces and dipped in extra-virgin olive oil or topped with tomatoes, bruschetta-style. It's also a great accompaniment to a light meal of soup or salad, and it makes a perfect sandwich bun when sliced in half horizontally.

SERVES 4 TO 6 / MAKES 1 LOAF

1½ cups plus 3 tbsp (415 ml) lukewarm water, divided

1 tsp sugar

2½ tsp (8 g) instant yeast

4 cups (500 g) all-purpose flour

4 tbsp (60 ml) extra-virgin olive oil, divided

1½ tsp (9 g) salt

¼ cup (30 g) black olives, pitted and halved

¼ cup (30 g) sun-dried tomatoes, roughly chopped

2 tsp (3 g) herbes de Provence, divided (see tip)

In a small bowl, combine 2 tablespoons (30 ml) of lukewarm water, the sugar and instant yeast. Set aside for at least 10 minutes, until the mixture is foamy.

In a large mixing bowl, combine the flour, 3 tablespoons (45 ml) of extra-virgin olive oil, 1½ cups (370 ml) of lukewarm water and salt. Stir in the yeast mixture, and knead until the dough comes together and doesn't stick to the edge of the bowl anymore.

Transfer the dough onto a floured work surface and knead for 15 minutes, until the dough is smooth and elastic. You can also use a stand mixer with a paddle attachment. Shape the dough into a ball.

Clean and grease the mixing bowl with 1 tablespoon (15 ml) of extra-virgin olive oil, and return the dough to the bowl. Cover with a kitchen cloth. Let rise at room temperature for 1 hour, or until doubled in size.

After 1 hour, return the dough to a floured work surface. Fold in the black olives, sun-dried tomatoes and 1 teaspoon of herbs. Flatten the dough to an oblong shape ¾ inch (2 cm) thick. Transfer to a large baking sheet lined with parchment paper, and cover with a kitchen cloth. Let rise for 1 more hour at room temperature.

(continued)

Fougasse aux Olives Noires et aux Tomates Séchées (Continued)

Preheat your oven to 430°F (220°C, or gas mark 7), with a rack in the middle.

Cut out six 3-inch (7.5-cm) slits in the dough, starting from the center and toward the edges into a leaf shape. Stretch out the slits with your fingers so they are 1 inch (2.5 cm) wide. Brush the fougasse with 1 tablespoon (15 ml) of water, and sprinkle with 1 teaspoon of herbs.

Place a small, ovenproof dish filled with water in the oven to create steam. Bake the fougasse for 25 minutes, until golden. Transfer immediately to a cooling rack. Enjoy warm or cool.

NOTE: *Substitutes for the black olives or sun-dried tomatoes can include: ¼ cup (25 g) of grated cheese; ¼ cup (35 g) of sliced chorizo; ¼ cup (20 g) of cooked bacon matchsticks; ¼ cup (57 g) of caramelized onions; 6 to 8 anchovies.*

FRENCH PANTRY TIP: *Herbes de Provence is a typical mix of dried herbs from Provence and usually includes savory, marjoram, rosemary, thyme, oregano and sometimes lavender too. You can find it in specialty stores or make your own at home. Use an equal amount of each herb and mix. Keep it in a sealed jar or tied-up pouch for months. Sprinkling 1 or 2 teaspoons of it in your stews, baked dishes or on grilled meats is the easiest way to bring fragrant Provençal flavors to the table.*

Gougères au Fromage

Baked Cheese Puffs

Originally from Burgundy, gougères are often served to accompany wine tastings in the region, but it's no wonder that they're such a beloved appetizer all over France too. They're cheesy, crisp and airy. It's simply impossible to stop at one. For me, making a batch of gougères is a must as a host.

When making them in France, I use Gruyère cheese, but in Canada I often reach for aged cheddar, as a more affordable option. Speaking of cheese, here's my trick for successful gougères: instead of folding the grated cheese into the dough, I top each dough ball with it, right before baking. This keeps the dough lighter, creating big holes inside, with a cheesy crackly exterior.

You can serve them on their own—they pair wonderfully with any wine or beer—or split them to fill with rolled-up charcuterie, or even more cheese!

MAKES 24 CHEESE PUFFS

1 cup (250 ml) water

⅓ cup (80 g) unsalted butter, cut in small cubes

1 tsp salt

¼ tsp nutmeg (freshly grated)

¼ tsp fresh ground black pepper

1¼ cups (155 g) all-purpose flour

4 large eggs

¾ cup (75 g) grated Gruyère cheese (or aged cheddar)

Preheat your oven to 390°F (200°C, or gas mark 6). Line two baking sheets with parchment paper.

In a medium saucepan, combine the water, butter, salt, nutmeg and ground pepper. Cover and bring to a boil. Simmer for 2 minutes. Remove from the heat, and immediately add in the flour. Stir in vigorously with a wooden spoon until a smooth dough forms. Return the saucepan to low heat, and keep stirring until the dough dries out and pulls away from the pan, about 2 minutes.

Remove from the heat again, and let cool for 1 minute. Beat the eggs thoroughly into the dough, one at a time. It is important each egg is fully incorporated into the batter before adding the next. If the dough separates, keep beating and it will come together again.

Using a cookie scoop or 2 tablespoons (about 15 g), drop tablespoon-sized balls of dough on the baking sheets, keeping them 1 inch (2.5 cm) apart. Sprinkle about ½ tablespoon (3 g) of grated Gruyère on top of each ball.

Bake for 30 to 35 minutes, until puffed and golden.

NOTE: *Make sure you have all the ingredients measured-out in front of you before you start: making the stove-top pâte à choux dough is fairly easy, but it's all about precise timing.*

Pissaladière

Onion, Anchovy and Black Olive Tart

This flagship recipe from the city of Nice, on the French Riviera, is one bold tart, with a scrumptious sweet and salty bite. Its name comes from pissalat, a condiment of pureed anchovies with spices and herbs, that would originally be spread on the dough before baking. Over the years, it has been replaced by whole anchovies for convenience. Traditionally this tart was made early in the morning by street vendors in Nice and sold to the early work crowd. It is still a favorite street food around the city, and it makes for a terrific appetizer too.

SERVES 8 / MAKES 1 TART

For the Crust

3½ tsp (14 g) instant yeast

2 tsp (14 g) honey

¾ cup plus 1 tbsp (200 ml) lukewarm water, divided

4 cups (500 g) all-purpose flour

1 tsp salt

2 tbsp (30 ml) extra-virgin olive oil (see tip)

For the Toppings

2 tbsp (30 ml) extra-virgin olive oil plus more for drizzling

4 large onions, peeled and thinly sliced

1 clove garlic, peeled and thinly sliced

1 dried bay leaf, crushed

3 sprigs of dried thyme

½ tsp salt

1-oz (30-g) can of anchovy fillets, drained (20 fillets)

16 pitted black olives

1 tsp fresh ground black pepper

Prepare the crust. In a small bowl, combine the instant yeast, honey and half the amount of the lukewarm water (⅓ cup plus ½ tablespoon, or about 100 ml). Set aside for 10 minutes; the mix will foam. Combine the flour and salt in a large mixing bowl, and dig a well in the middle. Pour in the yeast mixture along with the extra-virgin olive oil and the rest of the water. Knead for 10 minutes, until the dough is soft and smooth. Cover with a kitchen cloth, and let rise at room temperature for 2 hours, until doubled in size.

Prepare the toppings. Heat a large frying pan over medium heat with the extra-virgin olive oil. Add the onions, garlic, bay leaf, thyme and salt. Cook for 10 minutes, stirring occasionally, until soft and slightly caramelized. Cover with a lid and cook for 20 more minutes, stirring occasionally, until the onions are soft and melty.

Preheat your oven to 410°F (210°C, or gas mark 6), with a rack in the lower half. Spread out the dough onto a greased baking sheet, using your hands to press and stretch the dough. Spread the onions evenly onto the dough. Decorate with the anchovy fillets and black olives, creating a checkerboard pattern. Sprinkle with ground pepper, and drizzle with some extra-virgin olive oil.

Bake for 30 minutes, until the crust is golden. Cut into squares and serve immediately.

NOTE: *For a twist, try Pichade Mentonnaise, from the neighboring town of Menton. In this variation, the caramelized onions are paired with tomato sauce. I honestly can't choose which one I like best.*

FRENCH PANTRY TIP: *When cooking dishes from the South of France, always have a bottle of extra-virgin olive oil within arm's reach. Just like in most Mediterranean countries, it's the ingredient of choice in most dishes and even in some desserts, such as in the Pompe à l'Huile (Sweet Olive Oil Bread, page 142).*

Cervelle de Canut

Herbed Cheese Spread

This savory cheese spread is a specialty from the city of Lyon, and its name Cervelle de Canut means "silk weaver's brain." Don't worry, there is no brain involved whatsoever here! Many stories recount that it's named for the silk weavers of nineteenth-century Lyon who were called canuts. Starting work before dawn, the canuts would enjoy taking a mid-morning break at the bouchons, Lyon's bistros, and recharge with this scrumptious spread over crusty bread.

It's indeed a nutritious, hearty nibble that tastes creamy, fragrant and fresh all at once. Traditionally in France, the recipe is made with fromage blanc, a creamy soft cheese. But as a substitute when I am in Canada, I find that whole Greek yogurt works great for achieving the same satisfying taste and creamy texture. It's a great make-ahead appetizer that you can pop out of the fridge seconds before serving.

SERVES 4 TO 6

2 cups (570 g) plain whole Greek yogurt

2 tbsp (8 g) fresh flat-leaf parsley leaves, finely chopped

1 tbsp (3 g) fresh chives, finely chopped

1 tbsp (3 g) fresh tarragon, finely chopped

2 tbsp (30 ml) extra-virgin olive oil, divided

1 tsp minced shallot

1½ tsp (8 ml) red wine vinegar

1 tsp salt, or more to taste

¼ tsp fresh ground black pepper, or more to taste

Fresh herbs, for serving

Toasted baguette and/or crunchy raw vegetables, such as radishes or carrot sticks, for serving

In a large bowl, whisk together the yogurt, parsley, chives, tarragon, 1 tablespoon (15 ml) extra-virgin olive oil, shallot, vinegar, salt and ground pepper until incorporated and creamy. Taste, and season with more salt and pepper, if needed.

Line a double-layered cheesecloth over a fine-mesh strainer, and set it on top of a bigger bowl so there is a gap between the strainer and the bowl for liquid to drain. Transfer the mixture into the cheesecloth, and cover with plastic wrap. Refrigerate for at least 3 hours.

After 3 hours of straining, you will notice liquid at the bottom of the bowl and the yogurt will have firmed up to a cheesecake-like texture. Discard the liquid.

To serve, remove the cheesecloth from the strainer. Transfer the Cervelle de Canut to a serving bowl. Drizzle with 1 tablespoon (15 ml) of extra-virgin olive oil and additional herbs, if you wish. Serve with a baguette and/or vegetables.

FRENCH PANTRY TIP: *Fromage blanc is a fresh, creamy, soft cheese widely enjoyed in France. It is found in supermarkets in the yogurt aisle. It is often consumed as a dessert with fruits or a sprinkle of sugar, and finds its way into many baked goods. Fromage blanc is a rarer item to find in North America/U.K., so I always stock up on it if I ever happen to find it. As a substitute, I use Greek yogurt (or Quark or Skyr), like in this recipe.*

Barbajuans

Fried Ravioli

Barbajuans are succulent fried ravioli that are eaten as appetizers in the eastern part of the French Riviera and northern Italy. They're said to originate from the small village of Castellar, where locals would prepare them and sell them to markets in Monaco, and they are now the national dish. They vary in shape (triangle, square, round), but are commonly filled with Swiss chard, spinach, ricotta, Parmesan, onion and leek for a hint of sweetness, and then fried until perfectly crisp and golden. Some like to add rice or ham in the filling as well.

Rumor has it that one day a certain Mr. John found himself without a sauce for his ravioli and decided to fry them up. People loved them so much that they baptized them "Barba Juan," which translates to "Uncle John" in Monégasque, the local Ligurian dialect of Monaco.

SERVES 6 TO 8 / MAKES 16 TO 20 RAVIOLI

For the Dough

2 cups (500 ml) water

2 cups (250 g) all-purpose flour

3 tbsp (45 ml) extra-virgin olive oil

½ tsp salt

For the Filling

2 tbsp (30 ml) extra-virgin olive oil

¼ medium yellow onion, peeled and diced

⅓ leek, white part only, shredded

1½ cups (50 g / a big handful) fresh spinach leaves, chopped

2 Swiss chard leaves, green part only, stemmed and shredded

1 tsp dried oregano

¼ cup (60 g) ricotta cheese

⅓ cup (35 g) grated Parmesan, plus extra for garnish

1 egg white

Make the dough. Begin by heating up the water in a small saucepan. Remove it from the heat when you start seeing steam. Set aside for 2 minutes.

Meanwhile, place the flour in a big mixing bowl, and make a well in the middle. Add in the extra-virgin olive oil and salt, and start mixing by hand.

Slowly pour in the water in small additions, and continue mixing by hand until you get a soft ball that doesn't stick to the bowl. Don't add in all the water if it is not needed.

Wrap the dough in plastic wrap, and set aside to rest while you prepare the stuffing.

Make the filling. Heat the extra-virgin olive oil in a large frying pan. Sauté the onion and leek for 2 minutes, until they start to caramelize.

Add the spinach and Swiss chard and sauté for 4 to 5 minutes, until the greens lose most of their moisture.

Transfer the vegetables to a bowl. Mix in the oregano, ricotta, Parmesan and the egg white.

(continued)

Barbajuans (Continued)

¼ cup plus ½ tbsp (68 ml) vegetable oil, for frying

To assemble the ravioli, divide the dough into 4 equal pieces. Roll them out on a floured work surface into 4 long rectangular sheets, measuring about 4 x 14 inches (10 x 35.5 cm) long and ⅛ inch (3 mm) thick. You can do this by hand with a rolling pin, or with a pasta maker.

Drop ½ tablespoon (8 g) of filling about 1 inch (2.5 cm) apart all along two of the sheets of dough; you should be able to fit 8 to 10 dabs of filling mixture onto each sheet. When the two sheets are fully dotted, cover with the other two sheets of dough. Using your fingers, gently press the dough between each dab of filling, to firmly seal it. Cut the ravioli into squares, using a zigzag-edged pastry cutter or sharp knife.

Line a large plate with paper towels.

Warm the vegetable oil in a heavy pan over medium heat. To test if the oil is at the proper temperature, place the handle of a wooden spoon in the oil. The oil is ready when bubbles begin to appear around the tip of the handle. Fry the barbajuans in batches of about 5—not more, or they won't cook properly. Fry for 2 to 3 minutes on each side until crisp, puffed and golden.

Transfer the barbajuans to the paper towel–lined plate, and continue to fry the remainder in batches.

Serve immediately, topped with freshly grated Parmesan.

Entrées et Petits Plats

Starters and Casual Fare

Despite the cliché of the typical lengthy multi-course meal, the line between a proper first course, a street food bite and a lighter weeknight dinner is often blurred in France. Today, the French have a much more relaxed approach to eating, and long meals are often reserved for weekends.

This chapter focuses on quicker and simpler dishes, but the recipes remain as traditional as can be—some things the French will never compromise on. Each dish reflects the habits of a specific region. The practice of al fresco dining is perpetuated in the South of France with handheld meals such as Taloak au Bacon, Fromage et Poivrons (Corn Flour Galettes with Bacon, Cheese and Peppers, page 45), Crespéou Provençal (Provençal Layered Omelette, page 37) and Pan Bagnat (Tuna Salad Sandwich, page 50), all intended for enjoying outdoors. In the North, relaxed fare has a homier connotation, with the notorious Gratinée à l'Oignon (One-Pot French Onion Soup, page 33) and lesser-known Flamiche (Flemish Leek and Cream Quiche, page 34).

Although the decorum around dining and l'art de la table has been shifting toward a looser definition throughout the years, the rustic regional recipes are as important and popular as ever in France. At the table people find a sense of comfort and belonging. They connect with their roots, even if just for a moment—all while the rest of the world goes by at its crazy pace.

So here's to taking a pause, and to cooking and eating simple and unpretentious French fare . . . whether it's for lunch, dinner or anytime in between.

Gratinée à l'Oignon

One-Pot French Onion Soup

Bread, cheese and wine. Clearly, this quintessential French soup was bound to become one of the most sought-after dishes from the French repertoire.

Originally a food for the poor and simply made with onions and bread, home cooks adopted it and added cheese and alcohol for deeper flavors—wine in Paris, beer in the East, eau-de-vie or Champagne in Central France.

But it was truly in "Les Halles," Paris' former central food market, in the nineteenth century, that this soup earned its stripes. In this bustling quarter, it was served at early hours of the morning to a mixed crowd of market porters, yearning for a nourishing breakfast, and late partygoers, as a cure for hangovers. Today, for rather less prosaic reasons, La Gratinée is still enjoyed in Paris at night, and now throughout the day too.

This deliciously iconic soup is a breeze to re-create at home, and with just a few ingredients.

SERVES 4 TO 6

3 tbsp (45 g) unsalted butter

4 large sweet onions, peeled and thinly sliced

½ cup (125 ml) red wine

2 tbsp (30 ml) port wine or Cognac

8½ cups (2 L) beef stock

½ tsp freshly grated nutmeg

½ baguette (200 g), cut in ½" (1.3-cm)-thick slices

1 clove garlic, peeled and halved

2¾ cups (300 g) grated Swiss cheese (Emmental or Gruyère)

1 tsp fresh ground black pepper

In a large pot over medium heat, melt the butter and sauté the onions for 15 minutes, until tender and glistening. Turn the heat to high and sauté for 10 more minutes, until the onions are caramelized, stirring occasionally so they don't stick to the pan.

Turn the heat back to medium, and deglaze with the red wine and port wine. Let simmer for 5 minutes until half of the liquid has evaporated. Add the beef stock and nutmeg, stir and let simmer for about 30 minutes with the lid off.

In the meantime, preheat your broiler. Rub the baguette slices with the halved garlic clove. Lay the slices flat on a baking sheet. Broil for 2 to 3 minutes until lightly toasted.

Pour one-third of the onion soup into a deep casserole dish or ovenproof pot. Cover with one-third of the baguette slices and one-third of the grated cheese. Repeat this step twice, finishing with the last third of the grated cheese. Season with the ground pepper.

Place the casserole under the broiler for 5 minutes, until the cheese is melted and golden.

Enjoy immediately.

Flamiche

Flemish Leek and Cream Quiche

Quiche is always a crowd-pleaser and a must-have in your cooking repertoire. This traditional leek and cream quiche hails from the Picardy region in northern France, where leeks are popular in family meals. For some reason this dish is far less known than the notorious Quiche Lorraine with bacon, but I think it is just as tasty and satisfying: the sturdy crust embraces a savory flan loaded with sautéed leeks.

This recipe is quite versatile too. You'll often find flamiches complemented with caramelized onions, endives, cubed ham or cheese. If you get your hands on Maroilles, the iconic sharp-smelling cheese from Picardy, definitely add some to the filling!

A flamiche can be enjoyed warm or cold as a starter, or with a salad and a glass of white wine for a complete meal.

SERVES 8 / MAKES 1 (9-INCH [23-CM]) QUICHE

For the Pastry Crust

1¾ cups (220 g) all-purpose flour, plus extra for dusting

½ tsp salt

½ cup plus 1 tbsp (135 g) chilled unsalted butter, cut into small cubes

⅓ cup (80 ml) cold water

For the Filling

2 tbsp (30 g) unsalted butter

2¾ lb (1.3 kg) leeks, cut into 0.2" (½-cm) slices (white and green parts)

1⅓ cups (330 ml) crème fraîche

1 large egg plus 3 large yolks

¼ tsp freshly grated nutmeg

½ tsp salt

½ tsp fresh ground black pepper

To make the pastry crust, mix the flour, salt and butter with your fingers or pulse in a food processor, until you get a crumbly consistency and pea-size bits of butter are still visible. Add the water, and mix until the dough roughly comes together into a ball; do not overmix. Wrap the dough in plastic wrap, and chill for at least 30 minutes.

To make the filling, melt the butter in a large pan over medium heat. Sauté the leeks for 10 minutes, until soft and lightly caramelized. Transfer to a large bowl, and mix with the crème fraîche, egg and egg yolks, nutmeg, salt and ground pepper. Set aside.

Preheat your oven to 350°F (180°C, or gas mark 4). Grease and flour a 9-inch (23-cm) pie dish.

Take the pastry crust out of the fridge, place it between two large sheets of parchment paper and roll it out to a 12-inch (31-cm) circle. Unpeel the top sheet of parchment paper, and transfer the crust to the pie dish. Cut any excess pastry crust that hangs over the edge, and poke the bottom of the crust all over with a fork. Pour the filling evenly over the crust.

Bake for 40 to 45 minutes, until the crust is golden brown and the filling is golden. Transfer onto a rack, and cool for at least 15 minutes before serving.

Crespéou Provençal

Provençal Layered Omelette

Originally made as a portable lunch for fieldworkers, this crespéou is a succulent omelette cake and Provence staple. It perfectly embodies the local cuisine: high-spirited and colorful, made with simple techniques.

Just like a fougasse (page 17), a crespéou invites creativity. The idea is to cook open-faced omelettes, usually 4 to 6, and stack them up in a free-form tower of alternating colors and vibrant flavors.

After trying this recipe once, you can choose to mix-up each layer with ingredients of your liking. For Provençal flavors try: Swiss chard, zucchini or capers for the green layer; bell pepper for the red; shredded cod for the pink; tapenade or anchovies for the black. You can play with spices and herbs too: yellow saffron, red paprika, green basil . . . .

A crespéou is refrigerated overnight and served cold the next day. Perfect for alfresco eating, in true Provençal fashion.

SERVES 6 TO 8 / MAKES 1 CRESPÉOU

⅓ cup (80 ml) extra-virgin olive oil, for the pan, divided

For the Yellow Omelette
1 onion, peeled and thinly sliced

2 large eggs

1 tbsp (15 ml) milk

½ tsp fresh ground black pepper

¼ tsp salt

For the Red Omelette
2 large eggs

1 tbsp (25 g) tomato paste

½ tsp smoked paprika

¼ tsp salt

To make the yellow omelette, heat 1 tablespoon (15 ml) of extra-virgin olive oil in a large frying pan over medium heat. Cook the onion for 6 to 7 minutes until soft; set aside. Whisk together the eggs, milk, ground pepper and salt. Stir in the onions. Re-grease the hot frying pan with the 1 tablespoon (15 ml) of extra-virgin olive oil, and pour in the egg mixture. Over medium heat, cook for 3 to 4 minutes, flip and cook for 2 more minutes until the omelette is cooked through. Transfer onto a shallow plate.

To make the red omelette, whisk together the eggs, tomato paste, smoked paprika and salt. Re-grease the hot frying pan with a tablespoon (15 ml) of extra-virgin olive oil, and pour in the egg mixture. Cook for 3 to 4 minutes over medium heat, flip and cook for 2 more minutes until the omelette is cooked through. Stack the red omelette on top of the yellow omelette.

(continued)

Crespéou Provençal (Continued)

For the Pink Omelette
2 large eggs

1 (4.25-oz [120-g]) can of tuna, drained

½ tsp fresh ground black pepper

For the Black Omelette
2 large eggs

1 tbsp (15 ml) milk

½ cup (50 g) chopped pitted black olives

½ tsp fresh ground black pepper

For the Green Omelette
2 handfuls fresh spinach, chopped

1 clove garlic, peeled and chopped

2 large eggs

1 tbsp (15 ml) milk

¼ tsp salt

Repeat the same process for the pink and black omelettes, adding another tablespoon (15 ml) of extra-virgin olive oil to grease the pan if needed. Continue stacking the prepared omelettes one on top of the other.

To make the green omelette, add more oil to the pan if needed. Cook the spinach and garlic for 5 minutes until soft. Whisk together the eggs, milk and salt. Pour into the pan and cook for 3 to 4 minutes, over medium heat. Flip and cook for 2 more minutes. Place on top of the omelette stack.

Let the omelette cake cool to room temperature. Cover with plastic wrap, and refrigerate overnight.

The next day, unwrap and flip the crespéou onto a serving plate, and cut into wedges.

Mouclade Charentaise au Curry

Broiled Mussels in Curry Cream

In the seventeenth century, French ports along the Atlantic coast chartered vessels to the Indias to bring back goods and spices, importing curry spices to France for the first time. The fragrant mix was quickly adopted by the locals and is added to many traditional seafood recipes, such as this mouclade.

This dish from the southwestern coast of France is less known than the classic moules marinères. Yet, the melding of the mussels' salty sea flavors with the creamy curry sauce is as surprising as it is delectable. It's a great shareable starter or meal alongside some fries.

SERVES 4

2 lb (about 1 kg) mussels

1 tbsp (15 g) unsalted butter

2 shallots, peeled and finely chopped

1 clove garlic, peeled and finely chopped

6–7 sprigs of flat-leaf parsley, stemmed and chopped, plus extra for garnish

1 cup (250 ml) dry white wine

3½ tbsp (50 ml) Pineau des Charentes or dry wine (see notes)

½ lemon, juiced

½ cup (125 ml) heavy cream

1 large egg yolk

½ tbsp (3 g) curry powder (see notes)

Salt and fresh ground black pepper

Rinse the mussels thoroughly. In a large pot over medium heat, melt the butter. Add in the shallots, garlic and parsley. Cook for about 2 minutes, until the shallots are translucent. Add in the white wine, Pineau des Charentes and mussels. Stir, cover with a lid and cook, just until the shells open, about 3 to 4 minutes. Immediately transfer the mussels to a clean bowl to cool, and discard any mussels that did not open.

Strain the wine, discard the shallots, garlic and parsley, and return to the pot.

Whisk the lemon juice, heavy cream, egg yolk and curry powder together in a bowl. Gradually whisk it into the wine. Bring to a simmer and let it thicken to a creamy consistency, about 10 to 15 minutes, stirring occasionally. Preheat your oven's broiler.

Meanwhile, discard one shell from each mussel. Lay them flat on a baking tray, mussel meat facing up. Pour a teaspoon of the curry cream inside each mussel shell, and place the tray under the broiler for 1 minute. After carefully removing the hot tray from the broiler, sprinkle the mussels with a handful of fresh parsley, and season to taste. Serve immediately, in individual bowls or on a large serving tray.

NOTES: *A traditional mouclade requires a Pineau des Charentes (fortified wine), which I can find at the liquor store in Ontario. As a substitute, replace the Pineau with more dry white wine: add 1 cup plus 3½ tablespoons (300 ml) dry white wine in total.*

If you want to make your own curry powder from scratch, try this mix. For 1 small jar: 2 tablespoons (14 g) ground turmeric, 2 tablespoons (14 g) ground coriander, 2 tablespoons (14 g) ground cumin, 2 teaspoons (4 g) ground ginger, 1 teaspoon ground dry mustard seeds, 1 teaspoon fresh ground black pepper, 1 teaspoon ground cinnamon, ½ teaspoon ground cardamom seeds and ½ teaspoon cayenne pepper.

Salade de Pissenlits aux Lardons et aux Oeufs

Dandelion Salad with Bacon and Eggs

Dandelion greens grow all throughout spring in France and are enjoyed in many ways: sautéed, blanched or in soups. But in Alsace, it is in the form of this simple salad that they are most commonly eaten. The dandelion leaves are nutty with a pleasant bitterness, like radicchio. They pair so well tossed with rich lardons (small strips of bacon), creamy halved soft-boiled eggs, croutons and a simple vinaigrette.

Dandelion greens can be found in most grocery stores or local farmers' markets. But if you are unable to find them, feel free to substitute with other bitter greens, such as arugula, watercress or curly endive.

SERVES 4

For the Vinaigrette
½ shallot, finely chopped

2 tsp (10 g) Dijon mustard (see tip)

2 tbsp (30 ml) red wine vinegar

¼ tsp salt

¼ tsp fresh ground black pepper

¼ cup (60 ml) extra-virgin olive oil

For the Croutons
2 tsp (9 g) unsalted butter

2 cups (110 g) day-old baguette, cut into ½" (1.3-cm) cubes

¼ tsp salt

For the Salad
4 large eggs

½ lb (225 g) fresh dandelion leaves

6 strips bacon

Salt and fresh ground black pepper

To make the vinaigrette, in a small bowl, combine the shallot, Dijon mustard, red wine vinegar, salt and ground pepper. Let the mixture rest for 5 minutes to take the edge off the shallot. Slowly pour in the extra-virgin olive oil while continuously stirring with a fork to create an emulsion. Cover and refrigerate until ready to serve.

To make the croutons, melt the butter over medium heat in a skillet. When the butter sizzles, add the bread cubes and salt. Cook, while stirring frequently, until golden, about 3 to 5 minutes. Transfer the croutons onto a plate. As they cool, the croutons will crisp up.

Bring a pot of water to a boil. Plunge the eggs in and boil for 6 minutes (soft-boiled) or 12 minutes (hard-boiled), depending on how you like your eggs. Transfer the eggs to a bowl filled with cold water and a few ice cubes to cool completely in the ice-bath.

Wash, drain and place the dandelion leaves in a large salad bowl. Toss in the vinaigrette, and massage with your hands for 1 to 2 minutes. Arrange the leaves on serving plates.

Slice the bacon across the grain into short matchsticks, and fry them in a pan for 7 to 8 minutes until crisp. Sprinkle equal parts of the bacon strips and croutons onto the salad plates. Peel and halve the eggs, and place two halves on each plate. Taste and adjust the seasoning if needed.

FRENCH PANTRY TIP: *Dijon Mustard, named after the town of Dijon in Burgundy, France, is often used to create a typical French vinaigrette, to flavor and thicken sauces or simply to accompany meals, such as for a Choucroute Garnie Alsacienne (Alsatian Pork and Sauerkraut Stew, page 67).*

Taloak au Bacon, Fromage et Poivrons

Corn Flour Galettes with Bacon, Cheese and Peppers

The taloak is an iconic Basque-Country street food. This corn flour galette, resembling a Mexican tortilla, is quick and festive fare that locals enjoy on market days and in the streets during the day. They are commonly filled with a slice or two of bacon, a spicy sausage or slices of Jambon de Bayonne (Basque-style cured ham), topped with sheep's milk cheese (called Ossau Iraty) and cooked red peppers. But really, I think they are just as delicious with any seasonal fillings and local cheeses you can find.

Taloak are traditionally cooked in a wood-fire oven or "a la plancha," but a skillet or nonstick frying pan at home does the job just fine. You can prepare the galettes a few hours ahead, and simply reheat for a few seconds on each side in the pan before filling them.

SERVES 4 / MAKES 8 TALOAK

For the Galettes
1 cup plus 1 tbsp (125 g) corn flour (masa harina)

3 cups (375 g) all-purpose flour

½ tsp salt

Pinch of cayenne pepper

1 cup (250 ml) water, at room temperature

For the Filling
12–16 strips bacon

1 large red bell pepper, seeded and thinly sliced

¼ cup (30 g) firm sheep's milk cheese (such as Pecorino), thinly sliced

Salt and fresh ground pepper

Optional: a handful of fresh microgreens

To make the galettes, whisk together the two flours, salt and cayenne pepper in a large mixing bowl. Dig a well in the middle. Add the water in small additions, ¼ cup (60 ml) at a time, as you stir with your hands until the dough comes together into a soft ball and no longer sticks to your hands. Do not over-knead and do not add in all the water if it is not needed. Let the dough rest for 15 minutes.

Divide the dough into eight equal parts. On a floured work surface, roll out each part into a 6- to 7-inch (15- to 18-cm) circle, about 3 millimeters thick. Set aside under a damp kitchen cloth while you prepare the filling.

To make the filling, heat a frying pan or skillet over medium heat. When hot, add the bacon strips in a single layer and cook for 3 to 4 minutes until brown on the bottom. You will need to work in batches. Flip the bacon strips and cook for 2 more minutes. Keep the drippings in the pan; do not discard. Transfer the cooked bacon strips to a sheet of paper towel to absorb the excess grease. Cook the bell pepper strips in the bacon drippings, about 8 minutes, until tender. Transfer the bell peppers to a paper towel. Discard the drippings but do not wash the pan, as you want it to be still lightly greased for frying up the galettes.

Fry each galette 1 minute per side, until cooked and colored with light-brown spots. In the pan, garnish each with 1 or 2 strips of bacon, 5 to 6 strips of red pepper and 2 small slices of cheese. Season with salt and ground pepper, to taste.

Garnish with some microgreens (if using) for a little peppery crunch. Fold in half, and enjoy immediately.

Tourin à l'Ail

Garlic and Egg Drop Soup

My first year in Canada, I took part in a cooking competition and won the Jury's Prize with this soup—a staple recipe from the southwest of France. Naturally, I couldn't pass on the opportunity to include it in this book.

It is made with a whole head of garlic, but don't be scared: the garlic bite mellows out as it cooks, creating a well-balanced and soothing broth. It simply hits all the right notes: it's quick to make, incredibly fragrant and tasty, and great to ward off winter ills—and it cures hangovers!

With the last spoonfuls of this soup, you may be tempted to perform a chabrot. This peculiar custom from rural France calls for pouring red wine in the last of your soup and lifting the bowl to your lips to drink it, elbows planted on the table. A great symbol of the French conviviality, I think!

SERVES 4

1 head garlic (see note)

1 tbsp (15 g) unsalted butter

2 tbsp (17 g) all-purpose flour

6⅓ cups (1.5 L) chicken stock or vegetable stock

½ tsp salt

½ tsp fresh ground black pepper

3 large eggs

1 tbsp (15 ml) red wine vinegar

4 slices country-style bread, toasted

Peel the garlic cloves, and cut them in half lengthwise to discard any inner green sprouts. Chop the garlic in thin slices.

Melt the butter in large pot over medium heat. Add the garlic and cook for 15 minutes, stirring occasionally until soft and lightly caramelized. Stir in the flour and cook for 3 minutes. Slowly pour in the stock while whisking continuously to avoid lumps. Add the salt and ground pepper.

Separate the eggs. Add the vinegar to the egg yolks, and whisk into the garlic broth. Bring to a simmer, and whisk in the egg whites. Do not stop whisking until the egg whites cook and appear as stringy egg drops.

For serving, fill each bowl with soup and top with warm toasted bread slices.

NOTE: *Traditionally this soup is made with pink garlic from Lautrec, a little town in southwest France, near Toulouse. As a substitute, try to find local purple garlic as it's usually sweeter in taste.*

Trinxat de Cerdagne

Cabbage and Potato Galette

This trinxat—which translates to "chopped" in Catalan—is a gem of a recipe from Cerdagne, a region of the Pyrénées-Orientales mountains straddling France and Spain. Mashed potatoes are simply mixed with cabbage, fried in a skillet like a galette and garnished with bacon. It's easy and so satisfying, and a great way of using up leftover mashed potatoes too.

Like most mountain cooking, this recipe was born from a need to adapt to the region's climate and altitude. In the Catalan mountains, locals would make do with what can only grow at high altitude; in this case, potatoes and sturdy cabbages. The cabbages for this recipe were originally only harvested in the winter months, when bright green and slightly frosted. Nowadays, most recipes use Savoy cabbage.

In the spring, the cabbage can be replaced by peppery dandelion leaves. And at Christmas, trinxats traditionally get studded with raisins—it's surprising at first, but delicious.

SERVES 4 / MAKES 1 TRINXAT

3 large russet potatoes, peeled and cubed

Big pinch of salt

3 tbsp (45 ml) extra-virgin olive oil, divided

2 strips bacon

½ Savoy cabbage (¼ lb [113 g]), shredded (discard the outer leaves)

2 cloves garlic, peeled and crushed

Optional: ¼ cup (40 g) raisins (for the Christmas version)

Fresh ground black pepper

Cook the potatoes in boiling water with a big pinch of salt for about 15 minutes, until fork-tender. Drain and let cool for 5 minutes. Mash the potatoes with 2 tablespoons (30 ml) of extra-virgin olive oil, using a fork or a potato masher.

Heat a large skillet over medium heat. Cook the bacon strips until crisp, about 3 to 4 minutes on the first side and 2 minutes on the other. Reserve the bacon on a plate, and keep the rendered bacon fat in the skillet.

Add the shredded cabbage and crushed garlic to the skillet. Cook for about 15 minutes, until tender and slightly caramelized. In a separate bowl, mix in the cabbage with the mashed potatoes. Mix in the raisins (if using). Season to taste.

Add 1 tablespoon (15 ml) of extra-virgin olive oil to the skillet. Return the cabbage and potato mash to the skillet, and flatten it with the back of a large spoon to create a large galette. Cook for 5 to 10 minutes, until the bottom is brown and crisp. Top with the bacon strips, and serve immediately.

Pan Bagnat

Tuna Salad Sandwich

This typical sandwich from Nice is a favorite lunch in Provence that people grab along the way to work or the beach. It's not as well-known as the lovely Niçoise Salad, yet it embraces all its components between a bun. You can find it in most bakeries in Provence, where they often bake custom round buns for it.

A pan bagnat, meaning "bathed bread," is all about the "juice." The bread is first brushed with extra-virgin olive oil and vinegar so it becomes drenched for a tender chew. The assembled sandwich should then rest for two hours, for the bread to soak up the juices from the tomatoes and for all the flavors to blend beautifully.

Rules for the pan bagnat are quite strict—no ham, cheese or mustard!—but allow for a few add-ons, such as green onions, radishes or mesclun, a Provençal mix of young greens found in North America as Spring Mix.

SERVES 4 / MAKES 4 SANDWICHES

4 round ciabatta buns

1 clove garlic, peeled and halved

¼ cup (60 ml) extra-virgin olive oil

1 tbsp (15 ml) red wine vinegar

½ tsp salt

½ tsp fresh ground black pepper

½ can green fava beans (9.5 oz [270 g])

4 large ripe tomatoes, sliced into rings

2 green bell peppers, seeded and sliced

4 artichoke hearts, quartered (cooked, marinated or grilled)

4 large eggs, hard-boiled and sliced

16 black olives, pitted

1 can anchovy fillets, drained (12 fillets)

1 (5-oz [140-g]) can flaked tuna in oil or spring water, drained

16 fresh basil leaves

1 lemon, juiced

With a serrated bread knife, slice the buns in half horizontally. Remove some of the inside crumb to create more room for the fillings. Brush the garlic clove inside each sandwich bun, on both sides.

In a small bowl, whisk the extra-virgin olive oil with the red wine vinegar, salt and ground pepper. Brush a heaping tablespoon (15 ml) of the mixture inside each bun.

Drain the can of green fava beans. Now, place these ingredients in each bun, in the following order: 3 or 4 tomato slices, 6 or 7 green bell pepper slices, 4 artichoke quarters, 1 sliced egg, a handful of green fava beans, 4 black olives, 3 anchovy fillets, a heavy sprinkle of tuna (¼ of the can) and 4 basil leaves. Sprinkle with some lemon juice, and close the sandwiches.

Wrap the sandwiches tightly in plastic wrap, and refrigerate for 2 hours before enjoying.

Soupe au Pistou

Provençal Vegetable and Pistou Soup

This is the soup of late summer in Provence, when people head home from the market with baskets full of fresh basil, ripe tomatoes, beans of all kinds and plump zucchini.

Soupe au Pistou is very popular in Provence as it makes the most of seasonal vegetables in a delightful and versatile way—you can add or omit any vegetables. It is finished with pasta, which makes for a complete meal.

It's reminiscent of a minestrone, but what sets it apart is the pistou sauce, dolloped on top of each bowl and swirled. Not to be confused with the Italian pesto, the French pistou doesn't include pine nuts. It allows the basil to shine a bit more and is more affordable too. My advice: make sure to keep the jar of pistou within arm's reach on the table, as you'll want to add more as you go.

SERVES 4 TO 6

For the Soup

1 cup (200 g) dried beans (red, white or both), or 300 g of cooked, canned beans (drained)

3 tbsp (45 ml) extra-virgin olive oil

2 medium carrots, peeled and diced

2 cloves garlic, finely chopped

2 tsp (2 g) chopped fresh thyme

1 bay leaf

4 medium potatoes, peeled and diced

2 large ripe tomatoes, seeded and diced

2 small zucchini, diced

8 oz (225 g) green beans, tips removed and cut in quarters

1 onion, peeled and left whole, poked with 4 cloves

12⅔ cups (3 L) water

5 oz (140 g) small pasta (i.e., capellini, macaroni or anelli)

1 tsp salt, or to taste

1 tsp fresh ground black pepper, or to taste

For the Pistou

2 cloves garlic, peeled

Pinch of salt, plus more to taste

2 cups (40 g/1 bunch) packed fresh basil leaves, chopped

¼ cup (60 ml) extra-virgin olive oil

½ cup (50 g) Parmesan, grated

If using dried beans, soak the beans overnight covered in cold water. The next day, drain them.

In a large pot or Dutch oven, heat the extra-virgin olive oil. Add the soaked beans, if using, carrots, garlic, thyme and bay leaf. Sauté for 5 minutes. Add the potatoes, tomatoes, zucchini, green beans, onion and 12⅔ cups (3 L) of water. Bring to a boil and simmer for about an hour and a half, until the beans are tender.

Then, add the pasta to the soup with the salt and ground pepper. If using canned beans, add them now too. Simmer until the pasta is cooked.

Meanwhile, make the pistou. Using a large mortar and pestle or a food processor, pound the garlic to a paste with the salt. Add the basil leaves and pound them with the garlic until the mixture is a rough paste. Drizzle in the extra-virgin olive oil, and stir until combined. Stir in the grated Parmesan. Season to taste with salt.

For serving, remove the whole onion from the pot. Ladle soup in each serving bowl and top with a generous dollop of pistou.

Enjoy warm or cold.

Tarte Flambée or Flammeküeche

Thin-Crusted Onion, Bacon and Cream Tart

Flammeküeche always brings me back to my first memory of dining in an Alsatian restaurant. I watched these tarts being crisped over wood-fires, brought to our tables still sizzling, sliced hurriedly and devoured with our hands. I fell in love with the smell, the taste and the whole ritual.

Like the Préfou (page 13), this recipe was born from bakers testing the temperature of their ovens by throwing a disk of bread dough into it. They would then eat it with what they had on hand, giving birth to one of the most sought-after specialties from Alsace.

Cream, onion and bacon together are heavenly, but the crust is just as outstanding here. Making it at home requires some time but will truly go a long way. The dough must be rolled out as thin as possible without tearing, and baked in a very hot oven—this is how you will achieve the crackling crust with "flamed" edges.

SERVES 4 / MAKES 4 TARTS

For the Crust
2 cups (250 g) all-purpose flour

1 tsp salt

3 tsp (12 g) instant yeast

¾ cup (180 ml) lukewarm water

For the Topping
2 cups (480 ml) crème fraîche (see tip; for a lighter version, substitute the crème fraîche with fromage blanc or quark)

1 large sweet onion, peeled and thinly sliced

12 strips bacon, cut into ½" (1.3-cm)-wide sticks

½ tsp salt

½ tsp fresh ground black pepper

¼ tsp freshly grated nutmeg

To make the crust, in a large mixing bowl, mix together the flour, salt, instant yeast and water until combined into a rough ball. Cover with a kitchen cloth and let rise for 3 hours, at room temperature, until doubled in size.

Transfer the dough onto a floured work surface, and divide in four equal parts. Shape into four balls, cover with a kitchen cloth and let rise again, at room temperature, for 1 hour.

Preheat your oven to 570°F (299°C), with a rack and a baking sheet in the middle of the oven.

Transfer the dough balls onto four pieces of parchment paper. Roll them out to 11-inch (28-cm) diameter circles. Spread one-quarter of the crème fraîche (½ cup [125 ml]) on each circle, top with one-quarter of the onion and one-quarter of the bacon sticks. Season with salt, ground pepper and nutmeg.

Bake each tart with the parchment paper on the preheated baking sheet for 7 to 8 minutes, until the crust looks crisp and the edges are slightly browned. Enjoy immediately.

FRENCH PANTRY TIP: *I always have at least 3 pots of crème fraîche in my fridge at all times. As you will notice in this book, it is extensively used in French cooking. See: Poulet Vallée d'Auge (Cider-Braised Chicken with Apples and Mushrooms, page 59); Bisteu (Bacon, Onion and Potato Pie, page 80); Ficelle Picarde (Cheese, Ham and Mushroom Stuffed Crêpes, page 88). Crème fraîche is a soured cream from natural bacterial culture, containing 30 to 45% butterfat. Compared to sour cream, it is slightly less sour and tastes richer. Crème fraîche is often used to build sauces and in desserts.*

Repas en Famille

Family Meals

In this chapter, find the flagships of French regional cuisine, Sunday family meals and meals for big occasions. Most recipes are decades, sometimes centuries old, but have not aged whatsoever and are still the cornerstones of restaurants, bistros and home cooks.

These recipes reveal the cultural influences that shaped French cooking. In Alsace, German influences gave way to robust dishes such as Choucroute Garnie Alsacienne (Alsatian Pork and Sauerkraut Stew, page 67). In the north, Belgian influences led locals to adopt beer as a key ingredient. See, for example, Carbonnade de Lapin aux Spéculoos (Beer and Speculoos Rabbit Stew, page 91).

In the French Alps, Italian neighbors influenced recipes such as Oreilles d'Ânes ("Donkey Ears" Creamy Spinach Lasagna, page 79). And in Catalonia, the traditional Boles de Picolat (Catalan Meatballs in Tomato Sauce, page 68) surely has some Spanish flair. Some recipes are rural France through and through, and they only rely on humble and widely available produce—such as Frésinat Albigeois (Garlicky Pork and Potato Scramble, page 76).

Most of these family-style meals are best suited for weekends, when you can devote a few hours to being home. They require time, but not necessarily a lot of effort. You can simply keep an eye on your simmering pot or the oven, while going on with your other leisurely activities. These dishes are great for feeding large tables. But for the stews and casseroles, most locals will tell you they're even better reheated the next day.

In true French fashion, these meals are best enjoyed preceded by an apéro (Chapter 1) and followed by a homey dessert (Chapter 4).

Poulet Vallée d'Auge

Cider-Braised Chicken with Apples and Mushrooms

Named for the beautiful Vallée d'Auge in the heart of Normandy, famous for its lush green rolling hills, apple orchards and dairy farms, this recipe combines some of the best bounties of the region: butter, crème fraîche, apples, cider and Calvados.

The creamy, cider-spiked, apple-and-mushroom-studded sauce is incredibly flavorful and uplifting. It's quite versatile too! The chicken is often substituted for pork or veal, which makes this a staple recipe you'll want to make over and over again.

SERVES 4

5 tbsp (75 g) unsalted butter, divided

4 chicken pieces (breasts and/or leg quarters), skin on

Salt and fresh ground black pepper

1 shallot, peeled and minced

1 medium carrot, peeled and cubed

3½ tbsp (50 ml) Calvados (see tip)

1½ cups (375 ml) dry cider

6–7 sprigs of flat-leaf parsley, stemmed and finely chopped

4 cooking apples (900 g) (such as Honeycrisp, Braeburn or Jonagold), cored, peeled and each cut into 8 wedges

2⅔ cups (186 g) white mushrooms, chopped

1 tbsp (13 g) sugar

¾ cup plus 1 tbsp (200 ml) crème fraîche

Cooked white rice, for serving

In a large frying pan over medium heat, melt 2 tablespoons (30 g) of butter. Season the chicken pieces with salt and ground pepper on both sides, and add them to the pan. Cook until brown, about 6 to 7 minutes on both sides. Transfer the chicken to a plate.

In the same frying pan, cook the shallot and carrot for about 5 minutes until tender and glistening. Stir in the Calvados, cider and parsley, and use a wooden spoon to scrape all the bits off the bottom of the pan. Return the chicken pieces to the pan, bring to a boil and let simmer for 30 minutes with the lid on.

Meanwhile, in a separate frying pan over medium heat, melt 3 tablespoons (45 g) of butter. Add in the apple wedges and mushrooms, and sprinkle with sugar. Cook until the apples are fork-tender, about 20 minutes.

Remove the chicken pieces from the first pan, and keep them warm on a plate under foil. Let the liquid simmer with the lid off for another 10 minutes to reduce. Stir in the crème fraîche, and mix until fully incorporated. Stir in the apples and mushrooms, and adjust the seasoning if needed.

Place the chicken back into the pan, and serve with white rice.

FRENCH PANTRY TIP: *Calvados is an apple brandy produced in Normandy, distilled from cider made from specially grown and selected apples. Calvados is often served for apéro in Normandy, and used in the local cuisine to impart sweet flavors to meat dishes and desserts. It is also the basis of the trou Normand or "Norman hole." It is said that a small drink of Calvados in between courses of a long meal will ease digestion and reawaken the appetite.*

La Bréjaude

Winter Vegetable and Crushed Ham Soup

This Bréjaude soup, from the Limousin region in central France, takes its name from the word *bréjer*, which means "to crush" in the local dialect. In addition to crushed pork, it features chunky vegetables and is traditionally poured over bread, which makes for a robust bowl of soup that's perfect for cold winter days.

I find the key to a soup like a Bréjaude is the building of a good broth. It should be made from scratch—no store-bought stock here!—and in this case, made by simmering pork belly to melt the lard into the broth.

Now, the truth is, because a lard-based broth is rather fatty, this soup does not appeal to younger generations like it used to. To remedy this, I have switched pork belly for ham steaks, as they are much leaner, shred easier and impart just as much flavor to the broth. But if you're up for pork belly, please do!

SERVES 4

12⅔ cups (3 L) water

1 lb (454 g) ham steaks, cooked

1 small Savoy cabbage, sliced in big wedges

2 leeks, cut in ½" (1.3-cm) slices (white part only)

1 kohlrabi, peeled and cubed

2 carrots, peeled and cubed

3 cloves garlic, peeled

6 cloves

1 bay leaf

1 tsp salt

1 tsp fresh ground black pepper

4 medium-size potatoes, peeled and cubed

8 slices stale bread

In a large pot, bring 12⅔ cups (3 L) of water to a boil. Drop in the ham steaks, and simmer for 1 hour.

After 1 hour, transfer the ham to a plate or work surface, crush/shred it roughly with a fork and place it back into the water. Add in the cabbage, leeks, kohlrabi, carrots, garlic, cloves, bay leaf, salt and ground pepper. Simmer for 30 minutes. Add in the potatoes and simmer for 20 more minutes, or until the potatoes are fork-tender. Adjust the seasoning if needed.

For serving, place 1 or 2 slices of bread at the bottom of each bowl. Pour the broth on top along with the vegetables and meat.

Galettes-Saucisses

Buckwheat Crêpes with Pork Sausages and Caramelized Onions

The Galette-Saucisse is the ultimate street food in Brittany, particularly in the city of Rennes where it's a most beloved snack to grab before a match at the soccer stadium. No wonder, as it consists of two Brittany staples: a soft and nutty-tasting buckwheat crêpe wrapped around a grilled pork sausage. A taste of my home region at its best!

It's also called the Brittany Hot Dog, but traditionalists will shriek if they see you add any ketchup, mustard or relish. Caramelized onions are an acceptable topping. In fact, I think the saltiness of the pork sausage wrapped in the sweetness of the caramelized onions is a match made in heaven.

SERVES 6 / MAKES 6 CRÊPES

For the Buckwheat Crêpes

2 cups (250 g) buckwheat flour (see tip)

½ tsp salt

1 egg

1 cup (250 ml) water

2 tbsp (30 g) unsalted butter, divided

For the Filling

3 tbsp (45 g) salted butter

2 onions, peeled and finely sliced

6 medium mild pork sausages (about 1⅓ lb [600 g])

Salt, to taste

To make the buckwheat crêpes, in a large mixing bowl, sift together the buckwheat flour and salt, and make a well in the middle. Add the egg, and mix with a wooden spoon or spatula. Switch to a whisk, and slowly pour in the water, whisking continuously until the batter is smooth, with the consistency of heavy cream. Do not use all the water if it isn't needed. If there are any lumps, pass your batter through a fine-mesh strainer.

Heat a large nonstick frying pan over medium heat with 1 tablespoon (15 g) of butter. Pour in ⅓ cup (80 ml) of the batter, and swirl your pan quickly to completely cover the bottom. Cook until micro-bubbles form on top, and the underside of the crêpe is golden brown, 2 to 3 minutes. Loosen the edge of the crêpe with a rubber spatula, then with your fingertips, peel off the crêpe and quickly flip it. Cook for an additional minute. Slide your crêpe onto a plate, and cover with a dish cloth. Repeat, adding another 1 tablespoon (15 g) of butter to grease the pan if needed. Stack your crêpes onto the plate, always keeping them covered with a cloth.

To make the filling, melt 3 tablespoons (45 g) of butter into the pan over medium heat. Cook the onions for 13 to 15 minutes, until caramelized. Add the pork sausages, and panfry until cooked through, about 5 minutes per side. Season to taste.

For serving, wrap each sausage in a buckwheat crêpe with 2 to 3 tablespoons (28 to 42 g) of caramelized onions. Eat with your hands, just like a hot dog.

FRENCH PANTRY TIP: *A bag of buckwheat flour in your pantry is a staple in Brittany, where making and eating buckwheat flour crêpes is a huge part of the local lifestyle. Did you know that savory crêpes in Brittany are always made from buckwheat flour and are therefore gluten-free? Crêpes made with wheat flour are only meant to be garnished with sweet fillings. Find buckwheat flour in most natural food stores.*

Poulet Basquaise

Basque Braised Chicken with Peppers

This emblematic dish from the French Basque Country is a favorite of home cooks: it's a quick-braised chicken recipe simmered in a rich peppery sauce, along with some chorizo sausage for a spicy kick. It's easy to make and has a great burst of fiery colors and sun-kissed flavors.

One of the signature flavors of this dish comes from the Espelette pepper, a quintessential spice in Basque cuisine. This chile is solely grown in the Basque Country, but is widely available in its ground form in France. It can be found in specialty stores in the rest of the world, and you can purchase it online too. And if I ever happen to be out of it, I use a blend (see note), which closely re-creates the delicate, sweet smokiness of the Espelette.

SERVES 4

2 tbsp (30 ml) extra-virgin olive oil, divided

4 oz (115 g) chorizo sausage, cut into ¼" (6-mm)-thick slices

4 chicken leg quarters (1.5 kg), skin on

3 medium onions, peeled and sliced into half rounds

3 cloves garlic, peeled and minced

4 bell peppers (3 red, 1 green), seeded and cut into ½" (1.3-cm)-thick strips

2 tomatoes, diced

1 tbsp (25 g) tomato paste

2 tsp (4 g) ground Espelette pepper

¾ tsp crushed red pepper flakes

¼ cup (60 ml) white cooking wine

1 cup (250 ml) water

Salt and fresh ground pepper

Cooked white rice, for serving

In a large high-sided cast-iron skillet or Dutch oven, warm 1 tablespoon (15 ml) of extra-virgin olive oil over medium heat. Add the chorizo sausage slices and cook until browned, stirring occasionally, about 7 minutes. Transfer to a plate and set aside. Add the remaining oil to the skillet, and add the chicken leg quarters to the pan, skin-side down. Raise the heat to high, and cook until the skin is browned, about 7 to 8 minutes. Transfer the chicken to the plate with the chorizo; do not discard the oil in the skillet.

In the same skillet over medium-high heat, add the onions, garlic and bell peppers. Cook until tender and glistening, about 8 minutes. Stir in the tomatoes and cook until tender, about 7 minutes. Stir in the tomato paste, Espelette pepper, crushed red pepper flakes, cooking wine and water. Bring to a simmer, scraping up the browned bits from the bottom of the pan. Return the chorizo and chicken leg quarters to the skillet. Simmer for about 30 minutes, stirring occasionally, until the liquid has thickened. Remove from the heat, and add salt and ground pepper to taste. Serve with white rice.

NOTE: *If you can't find Espelette pepper, mix together 1 teaspoon smoked paprika, ½ teaspoon sweet paprika and ½ teaspoon cayenne pepper.*

Choucroute Garnie Alsacienne

Alsatian Pork and Sauerkraut Stew

Notoriously hearty, Alsacian cuisine heavily features influences from its neighbor, Germany. This results in exceptional recipes like this one: a fragrant feast of pork and sauerkraut stewed in white wine. One of my favorite stick-to-your-ribs comforting dishes that's perfect for cold days.

With four different types of pork meats and loads of aromatics, a choucroute garnie may seem like a big dish to take on. But trust me, once you finish your shopping, you've completed most of the work. It is a stove-top, one-pot meal that requires only a rapid prep, a quick sear of the meat and little attention as it slow-simmers.

I have my methods for simplifying the recipe: I use store-bought sauerkraut. I sear the meat in lard instead of duck fat. And I happily sneak in Italian sausages if I can't find kielbasa. That said, mustard and crusty rye bread on the side is non-negotiable.

SERVES 8

¼ cup (50 g) duck fat or lard

1 lb (454 g) double-smoked slab bacon, cut in 4 pieces widthwise

1 lb (454 g) Polish kielbasa, cut in 2" (5-cm) pieces

4 bratwurst sausages (¾ lb [340 g] total), cut in half

½ rack (1 lb [454 g]) baby back ribs, halved crosswise

2 cloves garlic, peeled and chopped

2 (28-fl oz [828-ml] each) jars sauerkraut, drained

2 bay leaves

5 cloves

½ tsp caraway seeds

1 tsp juniper berries

1 tsp whole black peppercorns

1½ cups (375 ml) chicken stock

1½ cups (375 ml) dry white wine (ideally, an Alsatian Riesling, Gewürztraminer or Pinot Gris)

6–7 medium-size potatoes, peeled and halved

Grainy mustard and rye bread, for serving

In a large Dutch oven (8 quarts [7.5 L] or larger), melt the duck fat over medium-high heat. Sear the meat in several batches, until browned: bacon, 3 to 4 minutes per side; kielbasa, 3 to 4 minutes per side; bratwurst, 2 minutes per side; ribs, 4 to 5 minutes per side. Reserve on a plate.

Add the garlic to the pot, and cook for 3 minutes. Thoroughly drain the sauerkraut in a fine-mesh strainer, and add it to the pot. Add the bay leaves, cloves, caraway seeds, juniper berries and black peppercorns. Stir with a wooden spoon until evenly warmed. Add in the chicken stock and white wine. Nestle the reserved meat in the sauerkraut, and bring to a simmer. Cover and cook for 1 hour and 30 minutes. Add in the potatoes, and cook for an additional 30 minutes until tender.

Serve on a large plate, with grainy mustard and rye bread.

Boles de Picolat

Catalan Meatballs in Tomato Sauce

Catalan cuisine is often thought of as Spanish, but the northern part of Catalonia is indeed French. This leads to an exciting mix of flavors in the local cuisine, as seen in this dish. The earthy meatballs and white beans are very French, but they're simmered in a rich, spicy tomato sauce studded with green olives, for some big Spanish flavors. Other components make the sauce truly unique, including cinnamon and dried mushrooms. Note that it's important to use dried mushrooms, not fresh ones, as they'll impart so much more flavor.

This dish is usually prepared over two days, since the white beans have to soak overnight. Using dried beans is preferred as they absorb more flavors and have a better texture. But frankly, once in a while, I happily rely on canned beans. And the cooked meatballs in the sauce are freezer-friendly, so you can easily turn this rustic and comforting recipe into a quick midweek dinner if you wish.

SERVES 6 TO 8

4 cups (2 lb [900 g]) dried white beans, or 4 (28-oz [796-g]) cans of cooked white beans (drained)

2 tbsp (30 g) dehydrated mushrooms

For the Meatballs

2 slices stale bread

½ cup (125 ml) milk

1 lb (454 g) ground beef

⅔ lb (300 g) ground pork

½ lb (225 g) ground veal

3 large eggs

½ bunch of flat-leaf parsley, stemmed and chopped

2 cloves garlic, peeled and chopped

½ tsp salt

½ tsp fresh ground black pepper

3 tbsp (45 ml) extra-virgin olive oil

Soak the dried beans in water overnight, if using, prior to making the recipe.

The day of, soak the dehydrated mushrooms in a bowl of warm water for 30 minutes. Drain and set aside.

To make the meatballs, soak the stale bread slices in the milk for 5 minutes and drain. In a large mixing bowl, combine the ground meats, bread, eggs, parsley, garlic, salt and ground pepper. Mix with your hands, and shape into small 1½-inch (3.8-cm) balls; keep your hands wet with cold water so they don't stick. Line the balls up on a clean work surface, tray or parchment paper.

In a large stove-top Dutch oven or casserole dish over medium heat, heat the extra-virgin olive oil. Working in several batches, cook the meatballs 2 to 3 minutes on each side, until lightly browned. Set them aside in a large plate or bowl, covered with foil.

(continued)

Boles de Picolat (Continued)

For the Sauce

½ onion (75 g), peeled and diced

1 large carrot (75 g), peeled and cubed in big chunks

1 tbsp (8 g) flour

1 (28-oz [796-g]) can of peeled tomatoes

1 tbsp (25 g) tomato paste

1 cup (250 ml) water

1 cinnamon stick

½ tsp red pepper flakes

½ tsp cayenne pepper

½ tsp salt

½ tsp fresh ground black pepper

3.5 oz (100 g) green olives, pitted

2 tbsp (30 ml) extra-virgin olive oil

To make the sauce, in the Dutch oven or casserole dish, add the onion and carrot and cook over medium heat for 3 to 4 minutes, until glistening. Add the flour, and mix with a wooden spoon until dry. Roughly chop the peeled tomatoes and add them to the pan, along with the juice from the can. Add the mushrooms, tomato paste, water, cinnamon stick, red pepper flakes, cayenne pepper, salt, ground pepper, green olives and extra-virgin olive oil. Stir, bring to a simmer and add the meatballs and soaked white beans.

Simmer on low heat for about 30 minutes with the lid on, and 30 minutes with the lid off, until the sauce has thickened and the white beans are tender. Taste and adjust the seasonings, if needed. Discard the cinnamon stick, and serve hot.

NOTE: *If using canned beans, only add them 10 minutes before the end of the cooking time.*

Brandade de Morue

Salt Cod and Potato Brandade

Brandade de Morue is originally a specialty from the city of Nîmes, in Occitanie, but it's much beloved all throughout France. In fact, I recall eating lots of it in Normandy, often served with a generous dose of crème fraîche sauce—so dear to Normandy cooks.

Its name comes from the word brandar, which means "stirring" in the Provençal dialect. And stirring—or more precisely, whipping—is exactly what you're in for here. Completely by hand as per tradition, the salt cod is emulsified with oil before getting folded into a potato mash. Brandade is traditionally smooth and creamy; although I personally like to keep some cod flakes visible for a chunkier texture.

I'll let you decide how you prefer it. Either way, it just begs to be enjoyed with crusty bread and a squeeze of lemon.

SERVES 6

1¾ lb (800 g) salt cod (see note)

1 bay leaf

5 whole black peppercorns

1 sprig of dried thyme

2–3 large starchy potatoes (i.e., russet), peeled and cubed

4 cloves garlic, peeled, halved and desprouted

½ tsp salt

1 cup (250 ml) milk (2% or whole)

1 tbsp (15 ml) crème fraîche

6–7 sprigs of flat-leaf parsley, stemmed and finely chopped

1 tsp fresh ground black pepper, divided

¼ cup (60 ml) extra-virgin olive oil

2 tbsp (30 g) salted or unsalted butter, divided

Crusty bread and lemon wedges, for serving

The day before cooking, rinse the salt cod. Soak it in cold water for 24 hours in the fridge, changing the water twice.

The day of, drain the cod. Transfer it to a large pot of boiling water with the bay leaf, peppercorns and thyme. Poach for 10 minutes. Remove the cod and allow it to cool. Keep the pot full of water, and discard the bay leaf, peppercorns and thyme.

In the meantime, place the potatoes with the garlic cloves into the same pot of boiling water. Add the salt and cook until fork-tender, about 15 to 20 minutes. Drain the potatoes and garlic, and mash with the milk, crème fraîche, parsley and ½ teaspoon of ground pepper.

Preheat your oven to 390°F (200°C, or gas mark 6).

Break the cod flesh into coarse shreds, and remove any bones. Keep the skin, which serves as a binder. Whip the cod with the olive oil until creamy—or leave some cod flakes still visible if you prefer a chunkier texture.

Fold the cod emulsion into the potato mash. Spread the brandade into a baking dish greased with 1 tablespoon (15 g) of butter and swirl the top with a fork. Break the remaining 1 tablespoon (15 g) of butter into tiny pieces and dot the brandade evenly, lodging pieces in the crevices. Sprinkle with the remaining ½ teaspoon of ground pepper.

Bake for 20 to 25 minutes, until golden. Serve hot or cold, with crusty bread and lemon wedges.

NOTE: *The salt cod must be soaked for 24 hours prior to making this dish.*

Macaronade Sétoise

Stuffed Beef Rolls in Tomato Sauce with Pasta

Macaronade is the traditional Sunday meal in Sète, a seaside town on the Mediterranean. It's a big, earthy pasta dish likely imported by the Italians who settled in the region in the eighteenth century.

Locals are very proud of it, and it's said every family has its own recipe. There are no strict rules here, but rather a method that you can follow with your ingredients of choice. The dish starts by making brageoles—also called "alouettes sans tête," meaning "larks with no heads." They are small beef rolls, stuffed here with bacon, garlic and parsley. Then, the tomato sauce is flavored with a few twists—I use orange juice, zest and paprika—and slow-simmered.

Finally, this dish must be served over pasta. As you probably guessed, the name macaronade derives from macaroni—but funny enough, you'll find it more often served with larger pastas, such as penne, spaghetti or in this case, strozzapreti.

SERVES 4 TO 6

1 bunch of flat-leaf parsley

2 cloves garlic, peeled and chopped

6 chuck-region beef slices (⅛" [2 mm] thick x 5" [12.5 cm] long x 2" [5 cm] wide; see note)

6 strips bacon

3 tbsp (45 ml) extra-virgin olive oil

1 onion, peeled and chopped

¼ cup (60 ml) red cooking wine

½ orange, zested and juiced

1 tbsp (25 g) tomato paste

1 (28-oz [796-g]) can of diced tomatoes

1 tsp paprika

2 tsp (12 g) salt

1 tsp fresh ground black pepper

11–14 oz (300–400 g) pasta, such as strozzapreti, penne or spaghetti

Grated Parmesan, for serving

Start by making the brageoles. Finely chop the parsley with the stems, and mix it with the garlic. Set aside in a small bowl. Lay the beef slices flat on a work surface. Lay a strip of bacon on top of each beef slice and then add about 2 tablespoons (30 g) of the parsley-garlic mix. Starting from the narrow end, roll up each parcel, keeping them as tight as possible. Tie with butcher's twine.

In a Dutch oven or large stove-top pot, heat the extra-virgin olive oil. Sear the beef rolls for 5 minutes on each side over medium heat, until lightly browned. Set aside on a plate, and cover with foil.

Add the onion to the remaining oil and cook for about 3 minutes, until glistening. Add the wine, orange zest and juice, tomato paste, tomatoes and the equivalent of the tomato can filled with water. Stir, add the paprika, salt and ground pepper and transfer the beef rolls back into the pot. Bring to a simmer, and cook for 45 minutes with the lid on and 45 minutes with the lid off, until the sauce has thickened a fair amount.

Cook the pasta until it is al-dente. Drain and stir it into the sauce.

For serving, lay the beef rolls on top of the pasta, cut off the butcher's twine and sprinkle with grated Parmesan.

NOTE: *Ask your butcher for slices from the "chuck area" of the cow, cut into the dimensions you need. Alternatively, you can pound the meat into ⅛-inch (2-mm)-thick slices yourself. Do not opt for the thin fast-fry beef strips as they are not suited for slow-simmering; they get quite tough.*

Frésinat Albigeois

Garlicky Pork and Potato Scramble

As you can tell by many recipes in this book, pork and potatoes feature heavily in French country cooking. That's especially true in this dish: the simplest scramble of pork and potatoes, garnished with loads of garlic and parsley. A Frésinat can make a great breakfast, lunch or dinner.

This Frésinat Albigeois is a specialty from the Tarn, in the southwest of France. On local farms, it was a tradition to make and serve this dish the day following the slaughtering of a pig, with all the leftover pieces not deemed suitable for making charcuterie, like the throat. Thankfully nowadays, modern versions of the recipe accept common cuts such as the loin or shoulder.

SERVES 6

1 tbsp (15 g) unsalted butter

3⅓ lb (1.5 kg) pork loin, cut in ⅓" (8-mm) cubes

3⅓ lb (1.5 kg) potatoes, peeled and cut in ⅓" (8-mm) cubes

¼ cup (60 ml) vegetable oil

1 tsp salt

½ tsp fresh ground black pepper

6 cloves garlic, peeled and sliced

1 bunch of flat-leaf parsley, stemmed and chopped

In a large frying pan, heat the butter over medium heat. Add the pork and cook for about 30 minutes with the lid on. When the pork is cooked through, remove the lid. Turn up the heat to high, and sear the pork for about 30 seconds, until crisp and golden. Transfer the pork to a serving plate and cover with foil to keep warm; leave the drippings in the pan.

Turn the heat back to medium. Add the potatoes to the pan, along with the vegetable oil, salt and ground pepper. Cook for 15 minutes, stirring occasionally so the potatoes don't stick to the pan. Add the garlic, parsley and pork, and cook for another 5 minutes until the potatoes are cooked through and crispy; the garlic is meant to be just barely cooked. Adjust the seasoning, if necessary.

Oreilles d'Ânes

"Donkey Ears" Creamy Spinach Lasagna

A comforting dish hailing from the French Alps, this spinach and béchamel lasagna is wittily named for the wild spinach originally used in this recipe. The spinach leaves are ready to be picked when they're the size and shape of donkey ears. These big leafy greens get stirred into a milky béchamel sauce, layered between crêpes, topped generously with hard mountain cheese such as Gruyère or Tomme and baked to perfection. The epitome of mountain cooking!

Now, in modern versions of this recipe, lasagna sheets often replace the crêpes, which I find convenient when I don't have time to make a batch of crêpes. The comforting effect of this dish remains the same: it's utterly tender and creamy, with a crackling cheesy top.

SERVES 6 TO 8

2 tbsp (30 g) unsalted butter, divided

12 cups (about 360 g) torn, raw spinach leaves

12 crêpes or 6 large sheets of lasagna, cooked (see note)

1 cup (100 g) grated hard cheese (such as Gruyère), divided

¼ tsp fresh ground black pepper

For the Béchamel Sauce

⅓ cup (80 g) unsalted butter

½ cup (63 g) all-purpose flour

1¾ cups (420 ml) 2% or whole milk

⅓ cup (33 g) grated hard cheese (such as Gruyère)

¼ tsp freshly grated nutmeg

¼ tsp fresh ground black pepper

½ tsp salt

Melt 1 tablespoon (15 g) of butter in a large pan over medium heat. Sauté the spinach for 3 to 4 minutes until cooked. Set aside. When cool enough to handle, squeeze out most of the excess moisture from the spinach.

To make the béchamel sauce, melt the butter in a small saucepan over medium heat. Add the flour, and stir with a wooden spoon until combined. Switch to a whisk, and allow the butter and flour mixture to cook for 1 minute. Slowly pour in the milk, whisking continuously to avoid lumps and until the consistency is creamy, about 1 minute. Whisk in the cheese until melted, about 1 minute. Then add the nutmeg, ground pepper and salt. Add the béchamel sauce to the spinach, and stir.

Preheat the oven to 350°F (180°C, or gas mark 4), with a rack in the middle.

Grease a 14 x 9–inch (35 x 23–cm) rectangular baking dish with 1 tablespoon (15 g) of butter. Lay 4 crêpes or 2 large lasagna sheets on the bottom. Cover with one-third of the béchamel-and-spinach mixture and ⅓ cup (33 g) of grated cheese. Repeat this step twice to create three layers, with the last ⅓ cup (33 g) of cheese on top. Sprinkle with ground pepper.

Bake for 30 minutes, or until golden brown on the edges.

NOTE: *If making the recipe with crêpes, go to page 88 for the crêpe recipe. Double the recipe to make 16 crêpes, only use 12.*

Bacon, Onion and Potato Pie

Featuring creamy sliced potatoes, salty bacon and caramelized onions all draped in a crisp puff pastry . . . I think we have a French comfort dish at its best here. Before becoming a regional household staple, this savory pie from Picardy was originally a farmer's dish, made with simple terroir ingredients. You can actually find it made in other regions: in the south, they call it a Flaouzou.

For a quick version of this dish, I'm happy to occasionally lean on store-bought pastry. For the potatoes, choose a starchy variety, like russet, which are great for baking. Make sure you slice them very thin and evenly—use a mandoline if you have one—so they become utterly tender, while the outside pastry grows flaky.

SERVES 8

4 strips bacon

1 onion, peeled and finely sliced

1 lemon, juiced

5–6 starchy potatoes (i.e., russet)

2 (13-oz [370-g]) packets ready-rolled puff pastry

¾ cup plus 1 tbsp (200 ml) crème fraîche

Salt and fresh ground black pepper

¼ tsp freshly grated nutmeg

1 large egg yolk, for the egg wash

Cut the bacon strips in half so you have 8 pieces. Fry them in a pan over medium heat until cooked through but not crisp; set aside. In the same pan, fry the onion for 3 to 4 minutes until glistening; set aside.

Prepare a large bowl filled with cold water and the juice of one lemon. Peel and thinly slice the potatoes. Drop them in the bowl of water as you go to prevent them from browning.

Line a deep 9-inch (23-cm) pie dish with parchment paper. Unroll the first sheet of pastry and place it on the bottom of the dish; don't worry about the edges that hang over the dish.

Drain the potato slices, spread them out on a clean tea towel and thoroughly pat them dry.

Arrange one-third of the potato slices on the pastry crust in an overlapping pattern and in an even layer. Cover evenly with half of the onion, half of the bacon and half of the crème fraîche. Season lightly with salt and ground pepper. Repeat the process once again: a third of the potato slices, half of the onion, half of the bacon, half of the crème fraîche, nutmeg, salt and ground pepper. Finish the top layer with the last third of the potato slices. Unroll the second sheet of pastry, and place it over the top of the filling. Press the edges together tightly to seal—removing any trapped air as you do so. Roll up the hanging pastry sheet edges together toward the center to create a thick outer rim.

Chill the pie for 30 minutes. Meanwhile, preheat your oven to 395°F (200°C, or gas mark 6), with a rack in the middle.

Brush the top of the pie with the egg yolk wash. With the tip of a sharp knife, score a 1-inch (2.5-cm) circle in the center of the pastry lid, for the steam to escape from while baking.

Bake for 1 hour and 30 minutes, or until the top looks crisp and golden. Let cool for at least 15 minutes before serving.

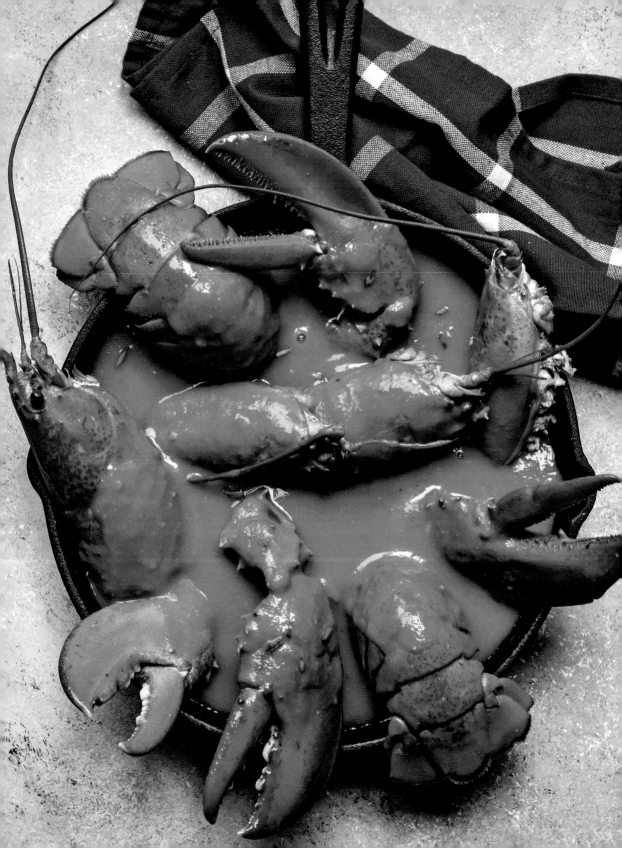

Homards à l'Américaine

Lobsters in American Sauce

While typically associated with Brittany, the renowned land of lobsters—and the best lobsters, if you ask me—there have been many theories about the provenance of this dish. The likeliest, I think, is chef Pierre Fraysse, who lived and worked in the United States, and who cooked this dish back in his Parisian restaurant for a table of American patrons. While the origin of this dish is likely not Breton, the people of Brittany have adopted it and made it their own. So much so that they don't call it American, but Armoricaine—from "Armor," the Celtic name for Brittany.

Lobsters are flambéed in Cognac sauce which may seem a bit sumptuous, but I promise you shouldn't be afraid of this recipe. If you get fresh lobsters, take them apart using the steps in the recipe; trust me, it's much easier than what you might imagine. Cook them in their shell for extra flavor, and you'll be set up for success.

SERVES 2 TO 4

5 tomatoes

2 large lobsters (1½–2 lb [680–910 g] each), uncooked (see note)

5 tbsp (75 g) unsalted butter, at room temperature, divided

3 shallots, peeled and diced

3 cloves garlic, peeled and diced

1 large carrot, peeled and diced

⅓ cup (80 ml) Cognac or other brandy (see tip)

Bring a large pot of water to a boil. Cook the tomatoes whole for 40 seconds. Transfer them immediately to a large bowl filled with cold water; keep the hot water in the large pot to re-use it later. When cool enough to handle, peel them by pulling the skin off with your fingers. Dice them roughly. Set aside.

If your lobsters are still alive, place the tip of a knife on the "cross" at the base of the head and insert quickly and forcefully to kill.

Bring the large pot of water back to a boil, and boil the whole lobsters, covered, for about 6 minutes. Drain and transfer them to a cutting board. When cool enough to handle, separate the front claws. Separate the small legs from the tail and discard, or keep them to make a stock. Separate the head/body from the tail. The roe (red eggs), if any, will be pulled out at the same time: keep them in a small bowl. Cut the head/body in half and discard the gravel pouches (black sand). Keep the tails whole.

Melt 2 tablespoons (30 g) of butter in a large saucepan or skillet with high edges over medium heat. Sauté the lobster pieces, shallots, garlic and carrot for 5 minutes. To flambé, using caution, pour the Cognac into the pan and turn the heat to medium-high, until the liquid reaches a light boil, 1 to 2 minutes. Remove the pan from the burner and set it on your counter or a heat-proof surface. Immediately, using a long match or barbecue lighter and approaching from the edge of the pan (not the middle), hold a flame within 1 inch (2.5 cm) of the liquid, until it lights on fire. Be sure to keep your face and hair away from the pan as it ignites. Quickly return the pan onto the burner, over medium-high heat, and shake it until the flames die out, which means no alcohol remains (about 10 to 15 seconds).

(continued)

Homards à l'Américaine (Continued)

2 bay leaves

2 sprigs of thyme

1 tsp cayenne pepper

3⅓ cups (788 ml) dry white wine

2 cups (475 ml) fish stock

2 tbsp (17 g) all-purpose flour

½ can tomato paste (2.75 oz [78 g])

5–6 stems of chives, chopped

Cooked rice, for serving

Add the tomatoes, bay leaves, thyme, cayenne pepper, wine and fish stock; it should cover the lobster. Bring to a slow simmer, and cook with the lid on for 20 minutes.

Meanwhile, combine the rest of the butter, flour, the one-half can of tomato paste and lobster roe to make a paste.

Transfer the lobster pieces to a plate, and cover with foil to keep warm. Bring the sauce to a high simmer over medium heat with the lid off. Reduce by half, about 20 minutes. Whisk in the roe paste, and simmer for 5 more minutes. Blend the sauce with a hand mixer or in a blender.

For serving, place the lobster pieces back into the sauce. Sprinkle with chives. Enjoy with rice.

NOTE: *This recipe works best with 1½- to 2-pound (680-g to 1-kg) lobsters, known as "halves," for a main course. Use "deuces," a bit bigger, for special occasions.*

FRENCH PANTRY TIP: *Arguably the most notorious French brandy, Cognac is made by double distilling white wines solely produced in the town of Cognac, in Charente-Maritime, and the surrounding regions. Cognac is beloved for its sweet fruity notes and unctuous texture, and it is often more approachable than Armagnac. It is widely available in North America, and you can enjoy it as a "digestif" after a big meal or to brighten up sauces.*

Petits Farcis

Sausage-Stuffed Baked Summer Vegetables

From Nice to Marseille, every family has their own take on Petits Farcis—meaning "little stuffed." Be it with pork or beef, with bread or rice, with parsley or basil, or with eggs or feta cheese, these sausage-stuffed vegetables are always a favorite in Provençal homes. They are enjoyed cold as an appetizer or hot as a main and are even better reheated the next day. This dish is all about smart use of your leftovers. It can be adapted to what you have on hand—ground or chopped meats, rice, stale bread—and made with vegetables that are in season.

SERVES 6

2–3 slices stale bread

½ cup (125 ml) milk (whole or 2%)

2 cloves garlic

5–6 sprigs of fresh flat-leaf parsley, stemmed

1 lb (454 g) ground sausage (pork and/or beef)

2 sprigs of dried thyme, stemmed

2 large eggs

Salt and fresh ground black pepper

2 tomatoes

1 red onion

1 zucchini

1 bell pepper (yellow, red or green)

1 eggplant

1 tbsp (15 ml) extra-virgin olive oil

To prepare the stuffing, crumble the stale bread in a bowl, and cover it with the milk. Let it soak for 1 to 2 minutes and drain. Peel the garlic cloves and chop them finely with the parsley. In a large bowl, mix the ground sausage, bread, garlic, parsley, dried thyme and eggs, with a pinch of salt and ground pepper.

Preheat your oven to 350°F (180°C, or gas mark 4), with a rack in the middle.

Cut the hats (tops) from the tomatoes and gently carve the insides out with a spoon. Sprinkle the insides with a pinch of salt, and place the tomatoes upside down on a linen or paper towel to absorb the juice. Peel the onion, cut a hat, and carve out the inside with a serrated spoon or small knife. Finely chop the removed flesh from the onion, and set aside. Divide the zucchini in two, widthwise, and cut each part in two again, lengthwise, to create four little boats. Carve out the inside of the zucchini boats, chop the removed flesh and set aside. Cut the hat from the pepper, and remove the inside/seeds. Remove the peduncle from the eggplant, cut it in half widthwise, carve out the inside and chop the removed flesh.

Heat 1 tablespoon (15 ml) of extra-virgin olive oil in a frying pan over medium heat. Sauté the chopped flesh of the tomatoes, onion, zucchini and eggplant. Cook until golden and mostly moisture-free, about 5 minutes.

Add the vegetable flesh to the stuffing and mix. Spoon the stuffing into all the hollowed vegetables, making sure they're well-packed. Place the hats back onto the vegetables, and place the vegetables standing in a baking dish, nice and tight. Season to taste.

Bake for 1 hour and 30 minutes. Near the end, if the vegetable hats are browning too much, place a sheet of foil on top. Allow the dish to rest for 30 minutes in the oven, with the oven turned off, before serving.

Ficelle Picarde

Cheese, Ham and Mushroom Stuffed Crêpes

Coming from Brittany, the birthplace of crêpes, I always made savory crêpes the traditional way, with buckwheat flour, until I discovered the Ficelle Picarde. This cheesy gratin of crêpes, stuffed with a mushroom cream and slices of ham, is a hit in its region, Picardy, and surely proves to Breton people that wheat flour crêpes belong with savory fillings too!

The filling starts with the making of a duxelles, a finely chopped mix of mushrooms and shallots, sautéed in butter and reduced to a crumbly paste. This simple preparation lends incredible flavors to the creamy sauce, and it raises this recipe from a classic ham and cheese crêpe to an elevated comfort dish.

SERVES 8 / MAKES 8 CRÊPES

For the Crêpes
1 cup (125 g) all-purpose flour

1 tbsp (13 g) sugar

Pinch of salt

2 large eggs

2 tbsp (30 g) unsalted butter, melted

1 cup (250 ml) 2% milk

1 tbsp (15 g) unsalted butter, at room temperature

For the Filling
3 shallots

6 cups (420 g) cremini mushrooms

4 tbsp (60 g) unsalted butter

Salt and fresh ground pepper

3 tbsp (45 ml) crème fraîche

8 slices Parisian ham, or best quality deli ham, thinly sliced

⅔ cup (70 g) grated Emmental cheese (or Gruyère, or aged cheddar)

To make the crêpes, in a large mixing bowl, sift together the flour, sugar and salt, and make a well in the middle. Add the eggs, and mix with a wooden spoon or spatula.

In a separate bowl, combine the melted butter and milk. Whisk the milk and butter into the crêpe batter, in small additions, whisking continuously until the batter is smooth with the consistency of heavy cream. If there are any lumps, pass your batter through a fine-mesh strainer. Cover the bowl with plastic wrap, and chill for at least 1 hour.

Heat a large nonstick frying pan over medium heat, with 1 tablespoon (15 g) of butter. Pour in ⅓ cup (80 ml) of the batter, and swirl your pan quickly to completely cover the bottom. Cook until micro-bubbles form on top and the underside of the crêpe is golden brown, 2 to 3 minutes. Loosen the edge of the crêpe with a rubber spatula, then with your fingertips, peel off the crêpe and quickly flip it. Cook for an additional minute. Slide your crêpe onto a plate, and cover with a dish cloth. Repeat and stack your crêpes onto the plate, always keeping them covered with a cloth.

To make the filling, peel the shallots and chop them very finely. Wash the mushrooms, and chop them very finely. Heat a large frying pan with the butter. Sauté the shallots and mushrooms until very soft, browned and all their juices have evaporated. Season to taste. Stir in the crème fraîche, and set aside.

Preheat your oven to 350°F (180°C, or gas mark 4), with a rack in the middle.

Lay a crêpe flat onto a plate. Top with a slice of ham and one-eighth of the mushroom cream. Gently roll up the crêpe, and place it in a 13 x 9–inch (33 x 23–cm) baking dish. Repeat with the other crêpes. Sprinkle the grated cheese evenly on the crêpes and season to taste. Bake for 15 to 20 minutes, until the cheese is melted. Serve immediately.

Carbonnade de Lapin aux Spéculoos

Beer and Speculoos Rabbit Stew

Unlike notorious French stews made with red wine (beef bourguignon, coq au vin, etc.), a carbonnade counts on strong Trappist ales to build a rich and silky gravy.

The alcohol completely evaporates after the simmering, so this is a 100% family-friendly dish—and with crushed cookies in the sauce, you won't want your kids to miss it!

You can definitely feel the strong influences from Belgian Flanders in this dish, where it's usually made with beef. In this typically northern French version, the use of rabbit and speculoos cookies adds new layers of richness, sweetness and warmth. It's a unique stew that is honestly so simple to make. I add root vegetables like turnips in my recipe as they absorb the sauce nicely and turn into little candy-like bites.

SERVES 4 TO 6

2 tbsp (30 g) unsalted butter

2 onions, peeled and diced

1 rabbit (about 2.7 lb [1.2 kg]), jointed (see note)

1 sprig of dried thyme

1 bay leaf

12 speculoos cookies, crushed (see note)

2 slices bread, shredded

½ cup (100 g) dark brown sugar

1 tsp salt

2 tsp (4 g) fresh ground black pepper

3 cups plus 3 tbsp (750 ml) Trappist ale (such as Chimay or another dark ale)

2 turnips, peeled and cubed

Fries, for serving

Melt the butter in a Dutch oven or flameproof casserole dish over medium-high heat. Add the onions and cook for 3 to 4 minutes, until glistening. Add the rabbit pieces, topped with the thyme, bay leaf, speculoos cookies, bread slices, brown sugar, salt, ground pepper and ale. Bring to a simmer, cover and cook for 1 hour.

Remove the lid, add the turnips and cook for another hour with the lid off, stirring occasionally until the sauce has the consistency of a thick gravy and the rabbit is fork-tender. Adjust the seasoning, if needed.

As per tradition, serve with fries.

NOTES: *Speculoos cookies are beloved and widely available in France. You can find them in many grocery stores in North America in the international aisle.*

Ask your butcher to joint the rabbit for you and debone the saddle. Discard the head.

Baeckeoffe

Three Meat and Vegetable Layered Stew

Along with Choucroute (page 67), Baeckeoffe is another savory pillar of Alsatian cuisine. This regional pot-au-feu includes tender pieces of meat, herbs, spices and seasonal vegetables simmered in white wine for several hours. This is a big, robust dish that is perfect to feed a large gathering. Baeckeoffe means "baker's oven" in Alsatian, as home cooks would prepare it and carry it to the local baker to be cooked in their oven (the only oven in the village, at that time). The key here is to dough-seal the lid of the pot to ensure it's completely hermetic and retains all the juices and aromas inside, just like a papillote.

SERVES 8

2 medium yellow onions, peeled and finely chopped

1 medium leek (whole), finely chopped

1 large carrot, peeled and finely chopped

2 cloves garlic, peeled and finely chopped

2 bay leaves

5 whole juniper berries

2 cloves

½ tsp celery seeds

1 sprig of dried thyme

5 sage leaves

1½ lb (680 g) boneless beef chuck roast, cut into 1¼" (3-cm) chunks

1½ lb (680 g) boneless pork butt, trimmed and cut into 1¼" (3-cm) chunks

1½ lb (680 g) boneless lamb shoulder, trimmed and cut into 1¼" (3-cm) cubes

3 cups (710 ml) dry white wine (ideally, an Alsatian Pinot Gris)

2 tsp (12 g) salt, divided

2 tsp (4 g) fresh ground black pepper, divided

1 tbsp (15 g) unsalted butter

4 lb (1.8 kg) potatoes (russet or Bintje), peeled and thinly sliced

2 cups (250 g) all-purpose flour

1 cup (250 ml) water

The day before cooking, place the onions, leek, carrot, garlic, bay leaves, juniper berries, cloves, celery seeds, thyme, sage, beef, pork, lamb and white wine into a large zip-top bag. Season with 1 teaspoon of salt and 1 teaspoon of ground pepper, seal and chill overnight.

The next day, grease a 9-quart (8.5-L) Dutch oven with the butter. Preheat your oven to 300°F (150°C, or gas mark 2), with a rack in the middle.

Lay a quarter of the potato slices at the bottom of the dutch oven. Top with one-third of the meat and vegetables; leave the liquids at the bottom of the zip-top bag. Repeat this step twice until no meat or vegetables remain, and finish with a fourth layer of potatoes. Pour the white wine marinade all over. Season with 1 teaspoon of salt and 1 teaspoon of ground pepper.

In a mixing bowl, combine the flour and water until they come together. Roll the dough into a long log, about 1 inch (2.5 cm) thick—long enough to go around the top rim of your dutch oven. Gently press the dough around the rim. Lay the lid on top, and press to seal.

Bake for 3 hours, until the dough around the lid is golden brown. Break the seal, discard the dough and serve.

NOTES: *The meat and vegetables need to marinate overnight in the white wine, so start the day before. A baeckeoffe customarily made use of odds-and-ends; so you can add other stewing meat cuts if you wish as long as the ratio of beef, pork and lamb remains the same. I sometimes throw a halved pig foot boasting collagen, to give a thicker texture to the simmering broth.*

Cotriade Bretonne

Brittany Fish Stew

Cotriade is a specialty from coastal Brittany, a region surrounded by the Atlantic where fresh-caught fish are the base of many dishes. Halfway between a soup and a stew, this broth with fish, potatoes and vegetables is so flavorful, yet very light—which makes it well suited to any season.

Unlike the notorious Bouillabaise (another fish stew from Marseille), the cotriade does not traditionally include any shellfish. It features a variety of white fish such as cod, haddock or any other fish you'd prefer, and it includes some richer ones, such as sardines and mackerel, to create a great mix of textures. It's finished with a drizzle of herb vinaigrette, which adds an agreeably tangy bite and beautifully brightens the entire dish.

To enjoy a cotriade as per tradition, sip the entirety of the broth first, and then eat the fish and potatoes with some crusty bread and butter.

SERVES 6

1.1 lb (about six 80–85 g whole fish) sardines and/or mackerel

12⅔ cups (3 L) water

1 large onion, peeled and cut in half

3 cloves garlic, peeled

1 bay leaf

3 sprigs of dried thyme

3 sprigs of curly parsley

4 tbsp (60 g) unsalted butter

2 large carrots, peeled and sliced in ¼" (6-mm) slices

2 leeks (white part only), finely sliced

18 little gold creamer potatoes, peeled

2 lb (about 1 kg) of various cuts of white fish (at least 3 different kinds; medium-firm: i.e., cod, haddock, turbot, gilt-head bream), cut into large 2–3" (5–7.5-cm) chunks

To make the fish broth, cut off the heads of the sardines and/or mackerel, discard of the insides and set the bodies aside. Place the heads in a large pot filled with 12⅔ cups (3 L) of water. Add the onion, garlic, bay leaf, thyme and parsley. Bring to a boil, and simmer for 30 minutes.

In the meantime, melt the butter in a large pot. Add the carrots, leeks and potatoes. Cook for 7 to 8 minutes, stirring occasionally, until the leeks are tender.

Drain the fish broth through a fine-mesh strainer; discard the fish heads, onion, garlic and herbs. Pour the broth in the pot over the carrots, leeks and potatoes. Bring to a simmer, and cook for 10 minutes. Add the white fish, and cook for 10 more minutes. Add the sardines and/or mackerel, and cook for 10 more minutes.

(continued)

Cotriade Bretonne (Continued)

For the Vinaigrette

2 shallots, peeled and finely chopped

½ bunch of curly parsley, stemmed and chopped

2 tbsp (30 ml) wine vinegar (red or white)

¼ cup (60 ml) neutral-flavored oil (grapeseed, canola or vegetable)

¼ tsp salt

¼ tsp fresh ground black pepper

Toasted bread and butter, for serving

While the fish is cooking, make the vinaigrette. In a small bowl, combine the shallots, parsley, vinegar, oil, salt and ground pepper. Set aside for at least 10 minutes to take the edge off the shallots.

For serving, place an equal amount of fish and potatoes in each bowl, and pour the broth over the top. Serve with the vinaigrette on the side and slices of toasted bread with butter.

Piperade aux Oeufs

Onion, Pepper, Tomato and Egg Skillet

At first glance, piperade can play the part of a French Ratatouille crossed with a spicy Middle Eastern shakshouka. But this quintessential dish from French Basque Country is, well, as Basque as can be.

It is a beloved local dish combining signature ingredients from the region: tomatoes, bell peppers, garlic, onion and hot chiles, enlivened with eggs and salty slices of melt-in-your-mouth Bayonne ham—the iconic local cured pork. It makes for a creamy mix of sweet and salty flavors, and its colors are also coincidently the colors of the Basque flag (red, green and white). It is an uncomplicated recipe, equally suited for breakfast, lunch or dinner.

Lastly, as with the Basque Braised Chicken with Peppers (page 64), a secret to the piperade is the Espelette pepper, which adds a sweet yet fiery kick. If you can't find any, use a blend of sweet and smoked paprika and cayenne pepper (see note on page 64).

SERVES 4

1 tsp unsalted butter

2 tbsp (30 ml) extra-virgin olive oil

2 medium yellow onions, peeled and thinly sliced

2 cloves garlic, peeled and thinly sliced

2 red bell peppers, cored and thinly sliced

2 green bell peppers, cored and thinly sliced

2 ripe tomatoes, diced

1 bay leaf

2 sprigs of dried thyme

½ tsp salt

1 tsp fresh ground black pepper, divided

½ tsp hot pepper flakes

2 tsp (4 g) Espelette pepper, divided

4 large eggs

4 slices Bayonne ham or prosciutto

Slices of toasted baguette, for serving

Preheat your oven to 400°F (200°C, or gas mark 6), with a rack in the middle.

In a large ovenproof dish or skillet over medium heat, melt the butter with the extra-virgin olive oil. Add the onions and garlic. Sauté for about 5 minutes, until soft and translucent. Add the bell peppers, and cook for 5 more minutes.

Stir in the tomatoes, bay leaf, thyme, salt, ½ teaspoon of ground pepper, hot pepper flakes and 1 teaspoon of Espelette pepper. Cook for 15 to 20 minutes, stirring occasionally, until the tomatoes are reduced to a puree.

Create four little wells in the mixture, and break an egg into each one. Lay a slice of Bayonne ham next to each egg. Bake in the oven for 10 to 12 minutes, until the egg whites are set.

Sprinkle with 1 teaspoon of Espelette pepper and ½ teaspoon of ground pepper. Serve immediately with the slices of the toasted baguette.

Saupiquet de Jambon et Crapiaux du Morvan

Ham Saupiquet with Potato Pancakes

Sitting at the heart of Burgundy, the Morvan is a small mountain massif well-known in France for its untouched nature and slow pastoral living. The local cuisine though does not get much attention, as it is rather simple and based on modest ingredients from local farms, such as ham and potatoes.

But I absolutely adore many dishes from the region. This Ham Saupiquet—seared ham slices decked with a creamy piquant sauce—and these little crapiaux pancakes made from mashed potatoes and yogurt are just two of the local specialties there. You won't traditionally find them served together in the Morvan, but I find that reuniting them on a plate makes for a succulent dish and a well-deserved tribute to Morvan cuisine.

SERVES 4/ MAKES 8 PANCAKES

For the Potato Pancakes
5 medium-size potatoes (about 1⅓ lb [600 g])

2 tsp (12 g) salt

¼ cup (75 g) Greek yogurt

2 large eggs

½ cup (63 g) all-purpose flour

5 sprigs of fresh dill, finely chopped

2 shallots, peeled and diced

1 tsp fresh ground black pepper

¼ cup plus 2 tbsp (90 ml) vegetable oil

To make the potato pancakes, peel and cube the potatoes. Bring a large pot of water to a boil, add the salt and potatoes and simmer for 10 to 15 minutes, until the potatoes are fork-tender. Drain the potatoes, and let them steam off for 5 minutes.

Transfer the potatoes to a large mixing bowl. Add in the Greek yogurt, eggs, flour, dill, shallots and ground pepper. Mash to a chunky texture.

Heat the vegetable oil in a heavy pan over medium heat. Scoop the mash onto the pan, using about ½ cup (120 g) for each pancake, and flatten lightly with the back of a spoon to a ½-inch (1.3-cm) thickness. Cook for 3 to 4 minutes on each side, until brown on the edges and crisp outside.

Transfer the pancakes to a paper towel–lined plate, and continue to fry the remaining mash in batches.

(continued)

Saupiquet de Jambon et Crapiaux du Morvan (Continued)

For the Ham Saupiquet

2 tbsp (30 g) unsalted butter, divided

1 shallot, peeled and finely diced

¾ cup (180 ml) white wine

1 tbsp (15 ml) wine vinegar

1 (5.5-oz [156-g]) can of tomato paste

1¼ cups (290 g) sour cream

½ tsp fresh ground black pepper

½ tsp salt

¼ tsp cayenne pepper

5 juniper berries

4 ham slices (about ¼" [6 mm] thick)

To make the ham saupiquet, melt 1 tablespoon (15 g) of butter in a medium saucepan over medium heat. Add the shallot and fry for 4 to 5 minutes, until lightly caramelized. Deglaze with the white wine and wine vinegar, bring to a simmer and reduce for 15 minutes; you should have about one-third of the liquid remaining. Stir in the tomato paste, sour cream, ground pepper, salt, cayenne pepper and juniper berries. Cook for 5 more minutes, and turn off the heat.

In a large frying pan, melt 1 tablespoon (15 g) of the butter over medium heat. Cook the ham steaks for 2 to 3 minutes on each side.

For serving, place each steak on a plate. Cover with a generous amount of warm saupiquet sauce, along with 2 or 3 potato pancakes.

Cassoulet

Meat and White Bean Casserole

From historic Languedoc, this cornerstone of southwestern French cuisine combines succulent bounties from the region: duck confit, a specialty from the Perigord; pork sausages, a specialty from Toulouse; and white beans, enjoyed all throughout the southwest.

Just like a Choucroute (page 67), a Cassoulet seems like a big dish to take on, but it actually requires more patience than skill. This recipe is a two-day process: from soaking the beans overnight, to cooking them in a fragrant broth, searing the meats and finally cooking the assembled dish for two and a half hours.

This is a dish to try over the weekend, when you can occasionally peek into your kitchen to check on the progress, while doing other activities. That said, it is one of my favorite dishes to eat and a most rewarding recipe to make. Well worth the patience!

SERVES 6

For the Duck Confit
2½ cups (590 g) coarse sea salt
2 duck legs (½ lb [225 g] each)
2½ cups (500 g) duck fat

For the Cassoulet
2¼ cups (415 g) dried cannellini beans
½ lb (225 g) pork skin
1 poultry carcass (duck or chicken)
2 onions, peeled and thinly sliced
2 carrots, peeled and roughly chopped
1 whole celery, roughly chopped
2 cloves garlic, peeled
1 bay leaf
3 sprigs of thyme
2 sprigs of rosemary
1 tsp salt
1 tsp fresh ground black pepper

To confit the duck legs, the day before cooking, cover the bottom of a plate with 1¼ cups (295 g) of salt. Lay the 2 duck legs flat on top, and cover with the rest of the salt. Cover tightly with plastic wrap, and refrigerate for 12 hours. The next day, rinse the duck legs thoroughly under cold water to remove all the salt. Pat dry with a clean towel.

Melt the duck fat in a large saucepan over medium heat. Add the duck legs, and slow simmer for 2 hours. Remove the pan from the stove, and let it cool to room temperature. Set it aside.

For the cassoulet, the day before cooking, soak the beans in 12 cups (3 L) of cold water. Let sit overnight at room temperature.

The day of, drain the beans, place them in a large pot and cover with cold water. Bring to a boil, let cook for 5 minutes and drain immediately. Place the beans back into the large pot, with another 12⅔ cups (3 L) of water, the pork skin, poultry carcass, onions, carrots, celery, garlic cloves, bay leaf, rosemary, thyme, salt and ground pepper. Simmer for 1 hour.

(continued)

Cassoulet (Continued)

4 medium mild pork sausages
(¾ lb [340 g] total)

½ lb (225 g) pork loin or shoulder

4 bacon strips (100 g), cut into
matchsticks

½ cup (60 g) bread crumbs

Meanwhile, scrape off most of the fat from the 2 confit duck legs. Warm them up in a large pan over low heat to melt the rest of the fat away; set aside. In the rendered fat, sear the pork sausages over medium heat until cooked through, about 5 minutes per side; set aside. Sear the pieces of pork until golden, about 5 minutes per side; set aside. Sear the bacon matchsticks until cooked but not crispy, about 5 minutes; set aside.

After 1 hour, drain the cooked beans; keep the broth. Discard the poultry carcass and remove the pork skin; set them aside. Stir in the bacon strips.

Preheat your oven to 320°F (160°C, or gas mark 3).

Lay the pork skins flat on the bottom of a casserole or large ovenproof dish; these are not meant to be eaten. Add one-third of the beans, the duck and pieces of pork. Top with the rest of the beans and nestle in the pork sausages. Pour in the broth until it just covers the meat and beans.

Cook for 2 hours with the lid off. While cooking, a thin crust will form on top. Every 30 minutes or so, break the crust with the back of a spoon, and shake the casserole gently to redistribute the juices. After 2 hours, sprinkle the bread crumbs evenly over the entire cassoulet. Cook for 30 more minutes, until the top is golden and crusty.

NOTE: *Because duck confit is not easy to find outside of France, I invite you to make your own. This is a simple two-day process, and duck confit can be kept for up to 3 months (refrigerated, in a sealed container), so you can make it the day before you cook a cassoulet or days earlier if you wish.*

Desserts Maison

Homey Desserts

While most French bakeries offer dazzling cakes and pastries—St. Honoré, Croquembouche, Mille-Feuille, among others—French home cooks have always adopted a more approachable method to baking. Making a dessert at home is first and foremost a moment of pleasure, full of the delightful anticipation of sharing it with friends and family.

The following desserts are traditional and very dear to home cooks. They are often the desserts of choice to wrap up a traditional Sunday family meal.

Naturally, they each feature cherished ingredients of their region: crème fraîche in Normandy, salted butter in Brittany, olive oil in Provence . . . . But you'll encounter a few surprising recipes too, such as the exotic Le Gâteau Nantais (Rum-Soaked Nantais Almond Cake, page 110) or the Andalucian-influenced Le Pastis Gascon (Flaky Armagnac Apple Pie, page 130) from Gascony—showcasing a unique part of that region's history.

Unlike the more renowned classic French desserts, these don't require piping bags, blow torches or advanced techniques. Often, a bowl, a spatula or whisk and a little elbow grease are all you need. These are the kind of recipes passed on from generation to generation, with each family often putting their own twist on it.

Bourdelots

Crusted Baked Apples with Red Currant Jelly

Normandy is France's apple region and naturally boasts an impressive apple-centric recipe repertoire. Of their sweet selection, these bourdelots are likely to be one of the simplest recipes—but one of the most delicious too.

I see this dessert as a lovely ode to treasured autumn fruits, parading them with no frills. Whole apples are simply filled with a dollop of red currant jelly, draped in a rich buttery pie dough and baked to perfection. The crust becomes crisp and golden, and the apples turn utterly soft and sweet inside, with a slight zing from the jelly. It's everything you love in a slice of classic apple pie, but bigger and better.

These Bourdelots are meant to be served warm with a big spoonful of crème fraîche, in true Normandy fashion. You could also switch the apples for pears—in which case, they are called douillons.

SERVES 6

For the Pie Crust
4 cups (500 g) all-purpose flour

⅓ cup plus 1 tbsp (78 g) sugar

1 tsp salt

1 cup plus 1½ tbsp (250 g) cold unsalted butter, cubed

2 large egg yolks

⅓ cup plus ½ tbsp (88 ml) cold water

6 medium-size baking apples (such as Honeycrisp, Braeburn or Jonagold)

2 tbsp (30 g) unsalted butter, divided

6 tbsp (120 g) red currant jelly, divided

1 large egg yolk, for the egg wash

6 tsp (24 g) sugar, divided, for sprinkling

Crème fraîche, for serving

To make the pie crust, combine the flour, sugar and salt in a large mixing bowl. Add the cubes of butter, and mix with your fingers until the texture is crumbly and pea-size bits of butter are still visible. Add in the egg yolks and mix to combine. Add the cold water, and mix to form a smooth ball. Wrap with plastic wrap. Refrigerate for 1 hour.

While the dough is resting, wash, dry and core the apples.

Preheat your oven to 350°F (180°C, or gas mark 4), with a rack in the middle.

Remove the dough from the fridge, unwrap and transfer onto a floured work surface. Divide into six equal pieces. Roll out each piece into a 9-inch (23-cm) diameter circle.

Place an apple at the center of a dough circle. Insert about 1 teaspoon of unsalted butter in the center. Then add 1 tablespoon (20 g) of red currant jelly; remove a tiny bit if it overflows. Gently bring up the edges of the dough over the apple to drape it entirely. Pinch the edges at the center to seal, and trim any excess dough you may have. With the excess dough, you can use a knife to cut out decorative leaf shapes and stick them at the top of the wrapped apple. Repeat with the other 5 apples.

Gently transfer the wrapped apples onto a parchment-lined baking sheet. Beat an egg yolk in a small bowl, and brush it evenly all over the apples. Sprinkle about 1 teaspoon of sugar over each apple.

Bake for 30 to 35 minutes, until the crust is crisp and golden.

Let cool 15 minutes, and serve warm with a dollop of crème fraîche.

Le Gâteau Nantais

Rum-Soaked Nantais Almond Cake

This popular regional cake from Nantes, in northwestern France, is a great testimony to this city's fascinating past. Snuggled between the river Loire and the Atlantic Ocean, the port of Nantes was a major stop on the spice trade route in the eighteenth century, with ships arriving from the Caribbean colonies bringing in bounties of goods for locals to discover. Vanilla and Antillean rum became common fixtures in the local cuisine and snuck their way into this local cake—which later became one of the culinary symbols of the city. It's satisfyingly dense and sweet and it's even better if you wait two to three days before enjoying it.

SERVES 8

½ cup plus 1 tbsp (125 g) salted butter, at room temperature, plus more for greasing

½ cup (63 g) all-purpose flour, plus more for dusting

¾ cup (150 g) sugar

1½ cups (150 g) ground almonds (see tip)

½ tsp salt

3 large eggs

1 tsp vanilla extract

¼ cup (60 ml) dark rum, divided

1¼ cups (150 g) powdered sugar

1½ tbsp (23 ml) water

Preheat your oven to 350°F (180°C, or gas mark 4), with a rack in the middle. Grease an 8-inch (20-cm) circular cake pan with ½ teaspoon of butter, and dust with 1 tablespoon (8 g) of all-purpose flour. Tap out the excess.

Cream together the butter and sugar, until fluffy. Add the ground almonds, flour and salt. Mix until just incorporated. Add the eggs and vanilla extract, and mix until smooth. Add 2 tablespoons (30 ml) of dark rum, and mix until incorporated.

Pour the batter into the prepared pan, and smooth the top out with a spatula. Bake for 45 minutes, until the cake is golden and a cake tester inserted into the center comes out clean.

Transfer to a cooling rack for 15 minutes, loosen the edges by running a knife around the cake, and flip it upside down onto a serving plate. Brush the top of the cake with the remaining 2 tablespoons (30 ml) of dark rum. Refrigerate for 30 minutes.

In a small bowl, mix the powdered sugar with the water to get a thick icing. Quickly spread it all over the cake. If needed, pass the cake under the broiler for 2 minutes for the icing to melt and cover the cake evenly.

Refrigerate for at least 4 hours, ideally overnight, before serving.

FRENCH PANTRY TIP: *Ground almonds (or almond flour; almond meal) is the base of many baked treats in France and I always keep a large bag of it in my pantry. Its most famous use is probably in the making of macarons, but it is extensively used in old-timey regional baking too. See, for example: the La Tarte Bourdaloue (Poached Pear and Almond Tart, page 119), Mirlitons de Rouen (Jam-Filled Almond Tartlets, page 129) and the Gâteau aux Macarons de Saint-Émilion (Original Macarons Chocolate Cake, page 121).*

Tarte au Fromage Alsacienne

Alsatian Cheesecake

Airier and lighter than its hefty American cousin, this French cheesecake—also called Käsekuechen—is a staple from the Alsace Region. Its sturdy crust encircles a pillowy filling tradtionally made with fromage blanc, but in Canada I substitute Greek yogurt and heavy cream for the same effect. The cake soufflés up in the oven and is then flipped upside down on a circular rack to cool—which maintains the cloud-like texture and completes its signature scalloped-top appearance.

SERVES 8 TO 10 / MAKES 1 CHEESECAKE

For the Pastry Crust

2 cups (250 g) all-purpose flour

½ tsp salt

½ cup (113 g) chilled unsalted butter, cubed, plus more for greasing the pan

1 large egg

¼ cup (60 ml) water

For the Filling

2¾ cups (785 g) Greek yogurt (10% fat or more)

⅓ cup (80 ml) heavy cream

⅔ cup (130 g) sugar

½ cup (63 g) all-purpose flour

½ tsp salt

4 large eggs (separate egg whites from egg yolks)

Powdered sugar, for garnish

To make the pastry crust, mix the flour, salt and butter with your fingers or pulse in a food processor, until you get a crumbly consistency and pea-size bits of butter are still visible. Add the egg and water, mixing just until the dough comes together. Shape the dough into a disk, wrap in plastic wrap and chill until firm—a minimum of 30 minutes.

Lightly butter a 9-inch (23-cm) springform pan. Take the dough out of the fridge, and roll to a 15-inch (38-cm) diameter circle. Transfer the dough into the springform pan, and ease it down to the base and up against the sides. Don't worry if the dough pleats on itself or cracks. You can fold the edges of the dough over the rim of the pan to keep them upright and patch cracks with excess dough; this crust is meant to be rustic-looking. Put the pan in the fridge while you prepare the filling.

Preheat your oven to 350°F (180°C, or gas mark 4).

To make the filling, whisk together the Greek yogurt, heavy cream, sugar, flour and salt. Add in the egg yolks, and mix until just incorporated. In a separate bowl, beat the egg whites to a firm peak. Gently fold the egg whites into the Greek yogurt–mixture with a spatula, until homogenous. The batter will be light and fluffy.

Take the pan out of the fridge and gently scrape the batter in, right to the edges of the crust. Bake for 40 to 45 minutes, until golden brown and a skewer comes out clean. The filling will have souffléd to about 1 inch (2.5 cm) above the top of the crust. Let the filling deflate to the same level as the crust in your oven, with the heat off, for about 15 minutes. Take the cheesecake out of the oven, and immediately flip it upside down onto a circular cooling rack. Remove the pan, and let the cake cool completely to room temperature before flipping it back over.

Chill for 1 hour. Sprinkle with a thin layer of powdered sugar before serving.

Kouign-Amann

Kouign-Amann

This specialty from the little town of Douarnenez, off the coast of Brittany, consists of a bread dough laminated with sugar and a lavish amount of butter, resulting in a flaky and utterly buttery cake. It is arguably the most popular and adored treat from Brittany, and is known to be quite an intricate recipe to make—which I think only adds to its "legend."

The creation of a Kouign-Amann is not labor intensive, but it does require time and precise measurements. A timer and ruler are recommended. By following the step-by-step photos and instructions, you will be able to replicate my perfect Kouign-Amann: a crusty outside, soft inside and perfectly caramelized edges.

SERVES 8 / MAKES 1 KOUIGN-AMANN

2 cups (250 g) all-purpose flour

1 tsp instant yeast

¾ cup (180 ml) lukewarm water

¾ cup plus 2 tbsp (200 g) unsalted butter, chilled, plus more for greasing the pan

1 tsp fleur de sel or sea salt flakes (see tip)

½ cup (100 g) sugar, plus more for dusting

In a large mixing bowl, or in the bowl of a stand mixer with a dough hook attached, combine the flour, instant yeast and water. Mix to combine into a rough sticky dough ball. Transfer to a lightly floured work surface. Knead for 10 minutes, until the dough is smooth and no longer sticky. Place the dough ball into a large bowl. Cover the bowl with plastic wrap, and leave it to rise in a warm, dry environment for at least 1 hour, or until it's doubled in size.

Slice the chilled butter into roughly ¼-inch (6-mm) slices, and place them on a plate to chill in the freezer for 30 minutes.

When the dough has doubled in size, transfer it onto a floured work surface. Roll it out to a 12 x 16–inch (31 x 40–cm) rectangle, with the long side facing you. Lay the butter slices in the middle of the dough to form a large square, leaving one-third of the dough exposed on both sides and about 2 inches (5 cm) at the top and bottom. Sprinkle the butter with the fleur de sel.

Fold the left and right sides of the dough over the butter so they are overlapping. Then fold the top and bottom sides of the dough into the middle as well. Roll the dough back out into a 12 x 16–inch (31 x 40–cm) rectangle, with the short side facing you this time. Fold the top and bottom sides of the dough into the middle so they are overlapping. Repeat the same rolling out and folding process once more, and wrap the dough rectangle in plastic wrap. Chill for 2 hours.

(continued)

Kouign-Amann (Continued)

After 2 hours, preheat your oven to 400°F (200°C, or gas mark 6), with a rack in the middle. Grease a 9-inch (23-cm) circular pan with a dollop of butter, and dust with sugar. Place the pan in the fridge.

Transfer the dough rectangle back onto a floured work surface, and roll the dough back out to a 12 x 16–inch (31 x 40–cm) rectangle, with the short side facing you. Dust the top evenly with ¼ cup (50 g) of sugar. Fold the top and bottom sides of the dough into the middle so they are overlapping, and roll the dough back out to a 12 x 16–inch (31 x 40–cm) rectangle, with the long side facing you. Dust the top evenly with the remaining ¼ cup (50 g) of sugar.

Roll the dough up tightly like a Swiss roll, slice it into eight even slices and place them into the pan in a flower-like pattern. Push down lightly to slightly flatten and stick the dough "petals" together.

Bake for 40 minutes, until the Kouign-Amann rolls have puffed up and become dark golden.

Transfer to a cooling rack for 1 minute, and then carefully tilt the pan to drain the excess butter that has melted at the bottom of the pan into a small bowl.

Unmold the Kouign-Amann, and keep it on the cooling rack. Brush the melted butter on top of the Kouign-Amann, for a glistening finish. Enjoy warm or cool.

For serving, slice the Kouign-Amann like a cake or tear off each individual roll.

FRENCH PANTRY TIP: *Fleur de sel—meaning "flower of salt"—is the thin crust of salt that forms at the surface of seawater when it evaporates. It is collected and sold in France as a highly sought-after product. You can use it as a table salt, and this is my secret weapon to make any dish or baked good's flavors pop. You can find it in North American/U.K. grocery stores, or opt for good-quality sea salt flakes for a more affordable option.*

La Tarte Bourdaloue

Poached Pear and Almond Tart

The Tarte Bourdaloue is one of the few typically Parisian desserts that has a rustic, country feel to it. It's simple to make at home, but it was born in the heart of Paris, on Bourdaloue Street to be exact, where pastry chef Fasquelle made it for the first time in the mid-nineteenth century.

The crisp pâte sablée is filled with tender poached pears and a flavorful almond cream filling, made from crème pâtissière and frangipane. For a quick version, or when pears are not in season, you can use canned pears in syrup; although I personally like to make my own poached pears, to bring out distinct spice notes.

SERVES 8 / MAKES 1 TART

For the Poached Pears
1 cup (200 g) sugar

1 cinnamon stick

4 cloves

3 star anise

4 medium, round pears (see note)

For the Pâte Sablée
½ cup plus 1 tbsp (75 g) powdered sugar

¼ cup (25 g) ground almonds

1¾ cups (220 g) all-purpose flour

½ tsp salt

½ cup (113 g) unsalted butter, at room temperature

1 large egg

For the Crème Pâtissière
2 large egg yolks

3¼ tbsp (40 g) sugar

2 tbsp (15 g) cornstarch

½ cup plus 1 tbsp (140 ml) milk (whole or 2%)

3½ tbsp (50 ml) heavy cream

½ tsp vanilla extract

To make the poached pears, bring 4 cups (1 L) of water to a boil with the sugar, cinnamon stick, cloves and star anise. Peel the pears, remove the stems, cut them in half and core them. Poach the pears for 15 minutes in the simmering syrup. Drain and set aside to cool.

To make the pâte sablée, combine the powdered sugar, ground almonds, all-purpose flour and salt. Add in the butter and egg, and mix with your hands to form a smooth ball. Wrap with plastic wrap and refrigerate.

To make the crème pâtissière, whisk together the egg yolks, sugar and cornstarch in a small bowl. In a medium saucepan, bring the milk, heavy cream and vanilla extract to a simmer. Slowly pour in the egg yolk–mixture. Whisk continuously for about 2 to 3 minutes, until the liquid thickens to a glistening cream. Remove from the heat, and let cool.

(continued)

La Tarte Bourdaloue (Continued)

For the Frangipane

½ cup (113 g) unsalted butter, at room temperature

1 cup (120 g) powdered sugar

1⅔ cups (158 g) ground almonds

2 large eggs

1 tbsp (15 ml) dark rum

2 tsp (9 ml) almond extract

2 tbsp (16 g) powdered sugar, for garnish

A handful of sliced almonds, for garnish

To make the frangipane, combine the butter, powdered sugar, ground almonds and eggs. Add in the dark rum and almond extract. Mix the frangipane with the cooled crème pâtissière.

Preheat your oven to 350°F (180°C, or gas mark 4), with a rack in the middle.

Take the pâte sablée out of the fridge, place it between two large sheets of parchment paper and roll it out to a 12-inch (31-cm) circle. Unpeel the top sheet of parchment paper, transfer the crust to a 9-inch (23-cm) pie dish and poke the bottom of the crust all over with a fork. Spread the filling evenly over the crust. Top with the poached and halved pears, with the outside of the pear facing up.

Bake for 40 to 45 minutes, until the crust is brown and the filling is golden. Transfer onto a rack, and cool for at least 2 hours before enjoying.

For serving, sprinkle with powdered sugar and sliced almonds.

NOTE: *Choose perfectly ripe pears for poaching: they won't poach well if underripe, and they will turn mushy if overripe. I like Bosc pears that hold a great shape and sweetness after being poached and baked, but the Anjou and Bartlett varieties work well too.*

Gâteau aux Macarons de Saint-Émilion

Original Macarons Chocolate Cake

You likely know French macarons as dainty little almond meringue cookies, sandwiched with buttercream or jam in the middle. But did you know their ancestors, the original macarons, are simple little sweet almond cookies—far easier to make and just as delicious?

Their origin dates back to the seventeenth century, from various French cities all fiercely claiming their invention, of course, including Saint-Émilion, in southwestern France. These macarons were made by the city's ursulines, using the almonds growing abundantly in their region. They are still very popular today, loved for their crisp shell and chewy insides.

And as if these macarons weren't irresistible enough, they are also used to create a decadent cake that is another specialty from the city. Built from layers of macarons and rich chocolate ganache, this Saint-Émilion's cake is an easy, yet absolutely decadent cake that is perfect for big occasions.

SERVES 8 / MAKES 1 CAKE

For the Macarons
2⅔ cups (320 g) powdered sugar

2 cups (200 g) ground almonds

½ tsp salt

4 large egg whites

For the Cake
¾ cup plus 2 tbsp (200 g) unsalted butter, at room temperature

¾ cup (150 g) sugar

½ cup plus 1½ tbsp (75 g) powdered sugar

¾ cup plus 2 tbsp (205 ml) milk (2%)

1 tsp vanilla extract

4 large egg yolks

7¾ oz (220 g) dark chocolate (70%)

To make the macarons, preheat your oven to 350°F (180°C, or gas mark 4), and line two baking sheets with parchment paper. Whisk together the powdered sugar, ground almonds and salt. In a large mixing bowl, beat the egg whites to a medium peak and gently fold in the dry ingredients, until just incorporated. The batter will be fairly thick.

Using a tablespoon or cookie scoop, spoon the batter onto the baking sheets into 24 small dollops, each 1 inch (2.5 cm) in diameter and 1 inch (2.5 cm) apart. Bake for 15 minutes. Lower the heat to 300°F (150°C, or gas mark 2) and bake for an extra 5 to 6 minutes, until the macaron rims are slightly golden. Using a spatula, transfer the macarons from the baking sheets to a cooling rack.

To make the chocolate ganache, in a large mixing bowl, cream together the butter, sugar and powdered sugar for 5 minutes until pale and fluffy.

Warm up the milk over medium-low heat with the vanilla extract in a small saucepan; you should still be able to safely dip a finger in it. Add the egg yolks, and whisk continuously until the milk thickens to a creamy consistency, about 2 to 3 mintues. Remove from the heat and set aside.

Melt the dark chocolate in a heat-proof bowl over a pot of barely simmering water. When melted, whisk it into the milk-and-egg mixture. Then stir this mixture into the creamed butter and sugar.

(continued)

Gâteau aux Macarons de Saint-Émilion (Continued)

2 tbsp (30 ml) Cognac or other brandy

2 tbsp (30 ml) water

To assemble the cake, line an 8-inch (20-cm) circular springform pan with parchment paper on the bottom and sides. Combine the Cognac and water in a small bowl.

Dip six macarons into the Cognac-water, line them at the bottom of the pan and spread out one-third of the chocolate ganache on top. Repeat this step twice, finishing with the last third of the chocolate ganache. Chill for at least 2 hours, until the ganache is set to a firm, fudge-like consistency.

Gently remove the cake from the pan, transfer to a serving plate and remove the parchment paper around it. Crush two to three of the remaining macarons, and sprinkle them on top for decoration. Serve immediately.

Pastis Landais et Crème Anglaise

Landes-Style Brioche with Crème Anglaise

Pastis means "cake" in the Gascon language, and you will find most baked goods named as such in the Gascony region. Two of my favorites include the Pastis Gascon (page 130) and the Pastis Landais, this rich, brioche-like cake flavored with vanilla, rum and, occasionally, orange blossom. Unlike most cakes, a Pastis Landais starts with the making of a levain, a pre-ferment of water, flour and yeast to develop the rising of the dough. This technique, typically used for breads and brioches, gives the cake an incomparably dense and melty crumb with a delicate crust.

SERVES 6 TO 8 / MAKES 1 PASTIS LANDAIS

For the Crème Anglaise
2 large egg yolks

3 tbsp (38 g) sugar

½ cup (125 ml) 2% or whole milk

½ cup (125 ml) heavy whipping cream

1 vanilla bean, split in half

For the Levain
1¾ tbsp (15 g) instant yeast

2 tbsp (17 g) all-purpose flour

⅓ cup (80 ml) lukewarm water

For the Pastis Landais
4 large eggs (2 whole eggs + 2 eggs with yolks and whites separated)

2¼ cups (280 g) all-purpose flour

½ tsp salt

½ cup (100 g) sugar

⅓ cup plus 1 tbsp (100 g) butter, melted, plus more for greasing the mold

2 tsp (8 ml) vanilla extract

1¼ tbsp (20 ml) rum

2 tbsp (24 g) pearl sugar (or 5 sugar cubes, coarsely crushed)

To make the crème anglaise, whisk together the egg yolks and sugar in a small bowl. In a medium saucepan, combine the milk and whipping cream. Scrape the seeds from the vanilla bean, and add them to the saucepan. Bring to a simmer and remove from the heat immediately. Whisking continuously, slowly pour the hot milk–mixture into the egg and sugar, and return to the saucepan over medium heat. Keep whisking for about 5 minutes until the crème thickens slightly. To test, dip a spoon in the crème and draw your finger across the back of the spoon; it is ready when the path remains clean. Remove from the heat, and transfer to a serving bowl; cover and chill until ready to serve.

To make the Pastis Landais, start by making the levain. In a small mixing bowl, combine the instant yeast with the all-purpose flour. Slowly mix in the lukewarm water, and let the mixture sit for at least 30 minutes. The mixture will bubble and become spongy.

In a large mixing bowl, break 2 whole eggs and 2 egg yolks; keep the 2 extra egg whites in a separate bowl. Add the all-purpose flour and salt, and mix until combined. Add the sugar, melted butter, vanilla extract and rum. Mix until fully combined and the batter is smooth and homogenous.

Beat the egg whites to firm peaks, and gently fold them into the batter. Using your hand or a large spatula, beat the batter vigorously for about 2 minutes—slapping it and stretching it out, to incorporate air. Cover with a kitchen towel, and set it aside to rise for 2 hours.

Preheat your oven 300°F (150°C, or gas mark 2), with a rack in the middle. Grease a fluted 8-inch (20-cm) brioche mold with butter, or use a round, high-edged mold and line it with parchment paper. Transfer the batter to the mold, and flatten the top with a spatula. Sprinkle the pearl sugar on top.

Bake for 40 minutes. Turn the oven heat down to 285°F (140°C). Bake for another 10 to 15 minutes, until the top is golden and a knife comes out clean. Serve warm with the crème anglaise on top.

Fontainebleau aux Fruits Rouges

Fontainebleau Mousse with Fresh Berries

As its name suggests, this elegant-looking dessert hails from the town of Fontainebleau, near Paris, famous for its château, which once belonged to the kings of France. This mousse of whipped cream and fresh cheese was supposedly invented in the nineteenth century by a local cheesemaker. Notice that I said supposedly, as mystery still surrounds the Fontainebleau—from its creator's name to its original recipe which some say includes egg whites and others crème fraîche.

Little pots of Fontainebleau are sold across France in fromageries (cheese shops), and over the years I've tasted all kinds of them to find my favorite, to re-create it at home. So, here it is. Perfectly airy and perfectly sweet. I love it to round a meal off on a lighter note.

MAKES 4 RAMEKINS

1 cup plus 1 tbsp (300 g) Greek yogurt or Quark/Skyr (see note)

1¼ cups (300 ml) whipping cream (+36%)

⅓ cup plus 1 tbsp (73 g) sugar

2 cups (250 g) fresh berries (blueberries, raspberries, etc.)

3 extra tbsp (38 g) sugar, for dusting

Line a double-layered cheesecloth over a fine-mesh strainer. Set it on top of a bigger bowl with room for liquid to drain. Pour the Greek yogurt into the cheesecloth, and cover with plastic wrap. Refrigerate for at least 3 hours.

After 3 hours of draining, you will notice liquid at the bottom of the bowl and the yogurt will have firmed up to a soft cheesecake-like texture. Discard the liquid.

Pour the whipping cream into a large bowl, and place it in the freezer for 10 minutes. Whip the cream to soft peaks, add the sugar and whip again until medium to stiff peaks form. Gently fold in the Greek yogurt.

Line double-layered cheesecloth into four small ramekins, and fill them with the Greek yogurt mousse. Refrigerate for at least 3 hours.

Thirty minutes before serving, lay the berries on a plate and sprinkle with the sugar. Shake the plate gently to ensure the berries are coated evenly. Place in the freezer for 30 minutes, as this helps the sugar to better stick to the fruit.

For serving, flip each ramekin onto a serving plate, gently peel off the cheesecloth and garnish with the now semi-frozen berries.

NOTE: *Making a Fontainebleau traditionally starts with "faisselle," a French-style fresh cheese similar to fromage blanc, only richer and firmer. Faisselle is hand-ladled into molds perforated with little holes to allow the whey to be drained. In Canada, I substitute the faisselle with more widely available thick Greek yogurt, Quark or Skyr, and drain it in a cheesecloth for a few hours.*

Mirlitons de Rouen

Jam-Filled Almond Tartlets

I don't know about you, but anything sweet and jam-filled inevitably brings me back to my childhood. Given the name of these jam-filled tartlets—Mirlitons, an old-time French flute played and enjoyed by children—I like to think these were invented to do just that: to resonate with our inner child.

A specialty from the city of Rouen in Normandy, Mirlitons are made of puff pastry filled with fruit jam and topped with a cream, sugar and ground almond mixture, which lends an unctuous frangipane-like texture.

The filling is traditionally made with French "Crème Fleurette," an unpasteurized liquid crème fraîche that usually contains 40% fat. However, I vouch that my version made with heavy whipping cream and a little extra fruit jam is just as irresistible. When fruits are seasonal, you can substitute fresh berries or bits of stone fruit.

MAKES 12 TARTLETS

1 (13-oz [375-g]) packet ready-rolled puff pastry

¾ cup (240 g) blueberry, raspberry or apricot jam, divided

1 cup (100 g) ground almonds

2 large eggs

½ cup (100 g) sugar

½ tsp vanilla extract

½ tsp orange blossom extract

⅓ cup (80 ml) heavy whipping cream

½ cup (55 g) slivered almonds

Preheat your oven to 350°F (180°C, or gas mark 4), with a rack in the middle.

Lay the puff pastry sheet flat on a floured work surface. Cut out twelve circles, 4 inches (10 cm) in diameter, and line them up gently inside a greased 12-muffin pan.

Drop a tablespoon (20 g) of fruit jam in in the center of each tartlet.

In a mixing bowl, combine the ground almonds, eggs, sugar, vanilla extract, orange blossom extract and heavy cream.

Pour the almond mixture into each tartlet, three-quarters of the way up; the filling will puff up as it bakes. Sprinkle each tart with slivered almonds

Bake for 25 to 30 minutes, until the pastry is golden and the filling is set. Enjoy warm or cool.

Le Pastis Gascon

Flaky Armagnac Apple Pie

The Pastis Gascon (sometimes called tourtière or croustade) is made of apple slices macerated in Armagnac, and super-fine pastry layers that are scrunched together on top for a spectacular rustic look. The thin pastry layers are reminiscent of Middle Eastern pastries, but the addition of local Armagnac brandy makes this into a true Gascony dessert.

The creation of an authentic pastis gascon is a rather labor-intensive exercise. The layers of pastry are traditionally rolled out paper-thin by hand on tables to dry overnight, and then brushed with goose fat. As a shortcut, many French home cooks like myself use phyllo sheets and butter instead, for a perfectly replicated flakiness and delightful crunch. By far, one of the most memorable apple pies I've ever had.

SERVES 6 TO 8 / MAKES 1 PIE

6 medium-size baking apples (such as Granny Smith, Honeycrisp or Jonagold)

½ cup plus 11 tbsp (230 g) sugar

⅓ cup (80 ml) Armagnac (see tip on page 133)

1 lemon, zested and juiced

½ orange, zest only

½ cup (113 g) unsalted butter, melted, plus more for greasing the pan

10 sheets phyllo dough, thawed (see note on page 133)

Peel, core and slice the apples in ¼-inch (6-mm) slices. As you cut the apples, place them in a large bowl with the sugar, Armagnac, lemon zest, lemon juice and orange zest. Toss the apple slices with your hands so they are evenly coated, and let them soak in the bowl for 1 hour.

Preheat your oven to 395°F (200°C, or gas mark 6), with a rack in the lower middle. Grease a 9-inch (23-cm) pie dish with butter.

Drain the apple slices, and reserve the Armagnac juice in a separate bowl.

Lay your first phyllo sheet on a work surface. Brush a thin layer of melted butter all over (about 1 teaspoon) and a thin layer of the Armagnac juice (about 1 teaspoon), and sprinkle evenly with 1 tablespoon (13 g) of sugar. Place the sheet at the bottom of the pie dish; the sheet's edges will hang around the dish by about 1 inch (2.5 cm). Repeat with 3 phyllo sheets, pilling each sheet on top of the other.

Spoon the apple slices on top of the phyllo in the bottom of the dish. Lay 5 more sheets of phyllo on top—buttered, juiced and sugared.

(continued)

Le Pastis Gascon (Continued)

Fold the edges of the phyllo sheets over the center, twisting them as you go so that they look irregular. Prepare the 2 last sheets of phyllo with butter, juice and sugar. Scrunch each sheet roughly and place them on top of the pie, to create a rustic look with peaks and folds. Gently brush the top with butter; do not press down on the phyllo sheets. Sprinkle with the last tablespoon (13 g) of sugar.

Bake for 30 minutes, until golden. About 10 minutes before the end, if the top looks like it's getting too browned, place a large piece of aluminum foil on top of the pie.

Transfer to a cooling rack and drizzle with the rest of the Armagnac juice. Serve it warm or at room temperature—but never reheated or it will soften the pastry sheets.

NOTE: *Phyllo sheets are delicate to handle and dry out easily and quickly. Keep them in your fridge up until you need them. When building the pie, place the sheets between a damp tea towel before you start handling them.*

FRENCH PANTRY TIP: *Armagnac is a barrel-aged eau-de-vie distilled from white wine and produced in Gascony in southwest France. It is slightly stronger in alcohol and in taste than the better-known French Cognac. Like most locally produced alcohol, it is a favorite for the apéro in Gascony, and it is often used in cooking in rabbit stews, terrines, paired with foie gras or in desserts.*

Tarte Bretonne aux Fraises et à la Crème

Strawberry and Cream Breton Tart

This is the seasonal dessert I look forward to making as soon as spring arrives: a delicious tart from northern Brittany where strawberries are exquisite and plentiful. The thick crust is a gâteau Breton—Brittany's most iconic cake, laden with the region's beloved delicacy: salted butter (see tip). As it's so irresistibly rich and buttery, a gâteau Breton is usually enjoyed on its own, but its firm structure makes it an outstanding crust in this dessert. It gets topped with crème pâtissière and fresh strawberries, left as they are.

The buttery gâteau Breton, the velvety crème pâtissière, the juicy strawberries . . . it is a bliss of perfectly combined textures and flavors. Plus, the assembly is as simple as it gets, so you don't need any decorative skills to make this rustic tart look as fabulous as it tastes.

SERVES 6 TO 8 / MAKES 1 TART

For the Gâteau Breton

¾ cup (170 g) unsalted butter, at room temperature, plus more for greasing the pan

1⅓ cups plus 1 tbsp (175 g) all-purpose flour

¾ cup (150 g) sugar

½ tsp fleur de sel or sea salt flakes

1 large egg plus 4 large egg yolks, divided

½ tsp vanilla extract (or ½ vanilla bean paste)

1 tsp milk

For the Crème Pâtissière

1 cup (250 ml) milk (2% or whole)

½ tsp vanilla extract (or seeds from ½ vanilla bean)

1 large egg plus 1 large egg yolk

3 tbsp (38 g) sugar

2 tbsp (17 g) flour

1½ tbsp (11 g) cornstarch

To make the gâteau Breton, preheat your oven to 350°F (180°C, or gas mark 4), with a rack in the lower middle. Grease a circular 9-inch (23-cm) cake pan. In a mixing bowl, combine the all-purpose flour, sugar and fleur de sel. Dig a well in the middle and add in the butter, the egg, 3 egg yolks and the vanilla. Mix with a wooden spoon until just incorporated. Transfer the thick batter into the prepared pan, and spread it evenly. Mix the remaining egg yolk with the milk, and brush it evenly onto the surface of the cake batter. Bake for 35 minutes, until golden. Transfer onto a cooling rack.

To make the crème pâtissière, in a medium saucepan over medium heat, warm up the milk and vanilla. Meanwhile, in a mixing bowl, whisk together the egg, egg yolk and sugar until lighter in color and fluffy. Whisk in the flour and cornstarch. When the milk is simmering, pour it into the egg mixture, and whisk until just incorporated. Transfer back into the saucepan, whisk occasionally and remove from the heat as soon as it begins to simmer. Pour into a clean bowl, and cover the crème with plastic wrap; the wrap should touch the whole surface of the crème to prevent a skin from forming. Set aside to cool.

(continued)

Tarte Bretonne aux Fraises et à la Crème (Continued)

For Topping

5½ cups (790 g) fresh strawberries

To assemble the tart, place the gâteau Breton onto a serving plate. Spread a thick layer of the crème pâtissière all over the top (about ¾ inch [2 cm] thick). Wash, drain and halve the strawberries; keep some stems if you wish, for a pop of green. Gently place them on top of the crème in a circular pattern.

FRENCH PANTRY TIP: *In the northwestern part of France, salted butter or "beurre salé" is often the way to go. The rest of France typically uses unsalted butter or "beurre doux," slightly salted butter or "beurre demi-sel," lard, duck fat or olive oil. Salted butter from France is about 3% to 5% more salted than the butter found in North America and the U.K. To re-create the same salty bite in recipes, I like to add a sprinkle of fleur de sel or coarse sea salt flakes to unsalted butter.*

Tarte au Caramel et aux Noix de Grenoble

Salted Caramel Walnut Tart

The city of Grenoble in southeastern France is known as the capital of the Alps, and to many, the capital of walnuts. Nestled at the foot of the mountains, the region exhibits valleys and hills of walnut trees producing the world renowned "Noix de Grenoble," highly sought after by chefs.

Naturally, this regional gem finds its way into many local specialties, including this luscious tart of walnuts and caramel. I love the twist of using salted caramel—the only way we enjoy caramel in Brittany—for a great mix of sweet, salty, crunchy and buttery.

SERVES 8 TO 10 / MAKES 1 TART

For the Pâte Sablée
¾ cup (90 g) powdered sugar

¼ cup (25 g) ground almonds

1¾ cups (220 g) all-purpose flour

½ tsp salt

½ cup (113 g) unsalted butter, at room temperature

1 large egg

For the Filling
¾ cup (150 g) sugar

2½ tbsp (53 ml) honey

2 tbsp (30 ml) 2% or whole milk

1 tsp lemon zest

¾ cup (180 ml) heavy whipping cream

¼ cup plus 2 tbsp (87 g) unsalted butter

½ tsp salt

⅔ lb (300 g) walnuts, whole

Fleur de sel or sea salt flakes, for sprinkling

To make the pâte sablée, combine the powdered sugar, ground almonds, flour and salt. Add in the butter and the egg, and mix with your hands to form a smooth ball. Wrap with plastic wrap, and refrigerate for at least 30 minutes.

Preheat your oven to 350°F (180°C, or gas mark 4), with a rack in the middle.

Take the pâte sablée out of the fridge, place it between two large sheets of parchment paper and roll it out to a 12-inch (31-cm) circle. Unpeel the top sheet of parchment paper, transfer the crust to a 9-inch (23-cm) pie dish and poke the bottom of the crust all over with a fork. Line the top of the crust with foil or parchment paper, and fill with pie weights or dried beans to keep the pie crust from puffing when baking.

Bake for 25 minutes until the edge of the crust is golden. Remove the pie weights and foil or parchment paper. Bake for 5 more minutes, until the center of the crust is slightly golden. Transfer to a cooling rack.

To make the filling, combine the sugar, honey, milk and lemon zest in a large saucepan over medium heat. Swirl the pan to dissolve the sugar. When the mixture comes to a boil, stop stirring and let it caramelize for 4 to 5 minutes. When you get a light caramel color, remove the pan from the heat and immediately stir in the whipping cream. It will bubble, so be careful and keep stirring until the cream is all incorporated. Stir in the butter and salt. Finally, stir in the walnuts and mix until they are all evenly coated. Transfer immediately into the pie crust.

Chill for at least 2 hours. Before serving, sprinkle with fleur de sel.

Kugelhopf

Alsatian Kugelhopf Cake

I discovered Kugelhopf as a child, in Alsace. It was served in gigantic slices in the morning, and I felt like I was eating dessert for breakfast. This cross between a brioche and a cake is moist, fragrant and not too sweet. Light and pillowy, Kugelhopf is the perfect canvas for butter, jam and honey. Assembling a Kugelhopf is easy, but the dough needs resting time. Start in the morning if you want the Kugelhopf to be ready by teatime.

SERVES 8 TO 10 / MAKES 1 KUGELHOPF

4 cups (500 g) all-purpose flour

2 tbsp (24 g) instant yeast

¼ cup (50 g) sugar

1 tbsp (22 g) honey

½ tsp orange zest

1 tsp salt

1 large egg plus 1 large egg yolk

¾ cup plus 2 tbsp (205 ml) milk

⅓ cup (80 g) unsalted butter, cubed, at room temperature, plus more for greasing the pan

1 tbsp (15 ml) vegetable oil

15 almonds, unsalted

½ cup (125 ml) water plus ½ cup (125 ml) Kirsch (see tip)

½ cup (75 g) raisins

Powdered sugar, for serving

In a large bowl, combine the flour, instant yeast, sugar, honey, orange zest and salt. Add the egg, egg yolk and milk. Stir with a wooden spoon or the paddle attachment of a stand mixer until the ingredients come together into a soft dough. Add in the butter in small additions, and knead until the butter is fully incorporated and the dough is soft, elastic and slightly sticky. Transfer the dough to a clean bowl brushed with the vegetable oil, cover with a cloth and let rise for 3 hours in a warm, dry place.

Meanwhile, grease the Kugelhopf pan with butter (see note). Lay the almonds at the bottom of the pan, in the crease of each ridge. Place the pan in the fridge for the butter to harden and the almonds to set in place. Combine the water, Kirsch and raisins in a bowl. Let them soak for 3 hours, and then drain the raisins and dispose of the liquid.

After the 3 hours, the dough should have doubled in size. Punch it with your fist to release the air and fold in the raisins. Shape the dough into a big ball, poke and enlarge a big hole in the middle to create a ring shape and place it in the bottom of the pan. Cover with a kitchen cloth and let rise for another hour in a warm, dry place.

Preheat your oven to 340°F (170°C, or gas mark 3), with a rack in the middle.

Bake the Kugelhopf for 35 to 40 minutes. Take it out of the oven, and immediately flip it upside down onto a cooling rack. Let cool to room temperature, and dust with powdered sugar before serving.

NOTE: *Traditional Kugelhopf molds are made of colorful enameled pottery with a signature ridged pattern. Sadly, they are hard to find outside of Europe, but coated-steel Kugelhopf pans can be found in specialty stores. Alternatively, a bundt cake pan will do the trick.*

FRENCH PANTRY TIP: *Kirsch is an eau-de-vie made from distilling fermented cherries (pulp, juice and pit included) popular in Germany, Austria, Switzerland and France. In Alsace, it is consumed for apéro or as a digestif, and often used in baking.*

Pompe à l'Huile

Sweet Olive Oil Bread

The Pompe à l'Huile is one of the "thirteen desserts" that are traditionally served on Christmas Eve in Provence, representing the Twelve Apostles and the Messiah. The dessert selections can vary, but often include an assortment of fresh, dried and candied fruits, nuts of all kinds, nougats and this sweet bread made with one of the region's prides: olive oil.

Come December in Provence, you will find it in most bakery stalls, but making your own *poumpo a l'oli* is also a cherished tradition for locals. Of course, they'll naturally tell you to use the best quality extra-virgin olive oil. It will lend an unctuous texture to this dense brioche-like treat with fruity aromas like none other.

They will also tell you: Always tear the bread into pieces with your hands. Never use a knife—for fear of bringing misfortune to the new year!

SERVES 8 / MAKES 1 LOAF

3¾ cups (470 g) all-purpose flour, divided

⅓ cup plus 2 tbsp (85 g) sugar, plus 1 tbsp (13 g) for topping

2½ tsp (8 g) instant yeast

1 cup (250 ml) lukewarm water

1 tbsp (22 g) honey

¾ cup (180 ml) extra-virgin olive oil, plus more for greasing the bowl

½ tsp salt

Place 1½ cups (190 g) of all-purpose flour, the sugar, instant yeast and the water in a large bowl. Stir well with a wooden spoon to combine. Let the mixture sit in a warm spot uncovered until foamy, about 30 minutes.

Stir in the remaining 2¼ cups (280 g) of all-purpose flour, the honey, extra-virgin olive oil and salt. Knead for about 7 to 8 minutes, until the dough becomes smooth and elastic. Grease a large clean bowl with 1 tablespoon (15 ml) of olive oil and place the dough in it. Cover with a kitchen towel, and set aside in a warm, dry spot to rise for 3 hours or until doubled in size.

Preheat your oven to 395°F (200°C, or gas mark 6), with a rack in the middle.

Transfer the dough to a large baking sheet lined with parchment paper, and roll it out to a 12-inch (31-cm) circle. Cut out five 2-inch (5-cm) slits in the dough, starting from the center and toward the edges into a five-leafed flower shape. Stretch out the slits with your fingers so they are 1 inch (2.5 cm) wide.

Bake for 15 minutes. Quickly remove from the oven, and sprinkle 1 tablespoon (13 g) of sugar evenly across the top of the bread. Bake for 10 more minutes, until golden.

NOTE: *This sweet olive oil bread is fantastic with a good fruit jam.*

Le Goûter
Afternoon Treats

Le goûter is unarguably an institution in France. A bit like the British teatime, goûter consists of sweet treats religiously eaten around 4:30 p.m. by children, as they leave school and flock to bakeries to pick up one or two pastries to keep them going through to dinner which is served around 7:30 p.m. in France. During the weekend, goûter is often enjoyed at home, with kids joining their maman or papa in the kitchen to bake a batch of delicious treats that the whole family will enjoy together. (Let's be real, adults do love goûter too.)

Because this is France, lots of children at bakeries unsurprisingly reach for a Pain au Chocolat (chocolate croissant), little Chouquettes (sugar-topped pastry puffs) or at home, one or two pieces of baguette stuffed with chocolate squares.

Throughout various French regions, you'll also see more singular treats in bakery stalls and on kitchen counters; and this chapter is devoted to these little treasures. In Brittany, big wedges of Far Breton (Prune Flan, page 148) are staples. On the other side of France, in French Catalonia, kids and adults alike love their Rousquilles (Lemon-Glazed Melt-in-Your-Mouth Cookies, page 155).

Like all regional specialties, these old-timey treats reflect the love affair each region has with certain ingredients. There are the spices and honey in Dijon's Nonnettes (Marmalade-Filled Honey Cakes, page 151). There is sugar in the North, found in the Gaufres Fourrées à la Vergeoise (Little Sugar Waffles, page 147). And there is the lemon and aniseed in Corsica in the Canistrelli au Citron et à l'Anis (White Wine, Lemon and Aniseed Cookies, page 160).

The variety of sweet regional treats is countless in France. You'll find one for every region, for every town, for every village. Frankly, one's lifetime may not be enough to taste them all. But here's my sweet little selection to get you started and to ease you into the delightful tradition of le goûter.

Gaufres Fourrées à la Vergeoise

Little Sugar Waffles

Cousins of Dutch stroopwafels, these little waffles hail from French Flanders, along the Southern border of Belgium. They are tender and stuffed with a luscious sugary buttercream.

Northern France has always had a love affair with sugar. In the nineteenth century, the first sugar refineries bloomed around the city of Lille, importing beet sugar from French colonies. Vergeoise, or sugar extracted from beets, became a common good in the region and led to the creation of sugar-centric treats like these waffles. The orignal recipe for these waffles did include vergeoise, but today you'll find them made with brown sugar, as it's now more common.

These waffles can be made in a classic thin waffle maker, although you'll notice I use a pizzelle maker which is easier to find in stores. The pattern is not as traditional, but the taste and texture are just the same—absolutely delicious!

MAKES 20 TO 22 WAFFLES

For the Waffles
½ cup (125 ml) milk

2½ tsp (8 g) instant yeast

4 cups (500 g) all-purpose flour

Pinch of salt

¼ cup (50 g) sugar

2 large eggs

⅓ cup plus 1½ tbsp (100 g) unsalted butter, at room temperature and cubed

For the Filling
1 cup (200 g) beet sugar or dark brown sugar

½ cup (113 g) unsalted butter, melted

To make the waffle dough, in a small saucepan, bring the milk to a lukewarm temperature over medium-low heat and stir in the yeast to dissolve. Let sit for at least 10 minutes, until foamy.

In a large mixing bowl, combine the flour, salt, sugar, eggs and milky yeast. Mix until just incorporated. Add the butter in small additions, continuously kneading until the butter is fully incorporated. Cover the bowl with a kitchen cloth, and let sit in a dry environment for at least 2 hours or until doubled in size.

After 2 hours, shape the dough into 20 to 22 balls (about 25 g each). Place them on a tray, cover with a kitchen cloth and let sit for 1 hour.

Meanwhile, make the filling. In a medium bowl, combine the sugar and melted butter until creamy.

Grease and heat a thin waffle iron. Place one dough ball in the iron, and bake until golden, about 2 minutes. Working quickly, remove the waffle from the iron, cut it in half horizontally, smear the inside with a generous dollop of the filling and close the two halves. Repeat with the rest of the balls.

Enjoy warm or cool.

Far Breton

Prune Flan

For many Brittany natives, myself included, Far Breton is a childhood favorite. Even today I inevitably search for a slice of it when entering a bakery in Brittany. This luscious custardy cake is a signature treat from the region and is widely enjoyed for breakfast, dessert and for le goûter. It is made with the simplest ingredients—milk, eggs, flour, sugar and prunes—all available year-round, and it is like most Brittany treats: unassuming, but rich and flavorful.

Some have created their own twist on it: using dried apricots, raisins and even Calvados-soaked apples in Normandy. But the most common version is this one, studded with rum-soaked prunes—quite dear in Brittany.

SERVES 6 TO 8 / MAKES 1 FLAN

20–25 pitted prunes (1¼ cup [220 g])

¼ cup (60 ml) dark rum (see tip)

2 tbsp (30 g) salted butter, divided

3¼ cups (760 ml) milk (2% or whole)

⅔ cup (130 g) sugar

4 large eggs

Pinch of salt

2 cups (250 g) all-purpose flour, sifted

Place the prunes in a bowl with the rum, and let soak for at least 30 minutes. Drain the prunes and reserve the rum.

Preheat your oven to 400°F (200°C, or gas mark 6), with a rack in the middle. Generously grease a 7 x 11–inch (18 x 28–cm) baking dish with 1 tablespoon (15 g) of salted butter.

In a large saucepan over medium heat, combine the milk, sugar and rum. Whisk until warm and the sugar has dissolved, about 2 minutes. Set aside.

In a large mixing bowl, whisk the eggs and salt. Slowly pour in the milk mixture and whisk until it is incorporated. Add in the sifted flour, and whisk until smooth and the consistency of a thin pancake batter. Pass the batter through a fine-mesh strainer to discard any lumps.

Place half of the prunes evenly along the bottom of the baking dish. Pour the batter in the baking pan up to three-quarters of the height of the pan. Add in the rest of the prunes; they will sink underneath the surface.

Bake for 35 minutes, until the edges are golden. Remove from the oven, and spread 1 tablespoon (15 g) of butter all over the Far. Bake for 10 more minutes. Take the pan out of the oven, transfer to a cooling rack and rest for at least 2 hours to allow the Far to firm up before serving.

FRENCH PANTRY TIP: *Often associated with the Americas, rum is in fact very prominent in French cooking, especially in the northwestern part of the country that took part in the eighteenth-century spice trade route. The French are also fond of rum for l'apéro, often in the form of a "ti-punch," a typical cocktail of rum, lime and sugar cane syrup, originating from the French Antilles and overseas territories.*

Nonnettes

Marmalade-Filled Honey Cakes

These plump little honey cakes with a citrus heart are a specialty from the city of Dijon. Yes, the same place that Dijon mustard comes from! It is said in the middle ages, the city's nuns would bake these treats in their monasteries—hence the name nonnettes which adorably translates to little nuns.

They're reminiscent of moist ginger breads, each filled with marmalade. Instead of using a piping bag, I top each one with a dollop of marmalade that sinks into the cake during baking. And if you're not fond of orange marmalade, you can substitute it for any fruit jam of your liking, or even one or two chocolate squares. Last but not least, because of the moisture from the honey and the spiced fragrance that develops over time, a nonette is best enjoyed the next day. It will be hard to wait, but you won't regret it!

MAKES 12 NONNETTES

⅔ cup (160 ml) water

½ cup plus 1 tbsp (200 g) honey

⅓ cup (72 g) brown sugar

⅓ cup (80 g) unsalted butter

½ tsp ground cinnamon

¼ tsp ginger powder

¼ tsp grated nutmeg

1 star anise

3 cloves

1 cup (105 g) rye flour

1⅓ cups plus 1 tbsp (175 g) all-purpose flour

1 tsp baking soda

½ tsp salt

6 tbsp (120 g) orange marmalade, divided

Preheat your oven to 390°F (200°C, or gas mark 6), with a rack in the middle.

In a medium saucepan over low-medium heat, combine the water, honey, brown sugar, butter, cinnamon, ginger powder, nutmeg, star anise and cloves. Stir until the butter has completely melted, about 3 minutes, then turn off the heat and let the pan sit on the stove.

In a large mixing bowl, whisk together the two flours, baking soda and salt.

Discard the star anise and cloves from the saucepan. Stir the honey mixture into the dry ingredients until combined. Divide the batter into a 12-muffin pan, lined with muffin cups.

Top each with a heaped ½ tablespoon (10 g) of orange marmalade, and push it in slightly so the marmalade sinks in.

Bake for 20 minutes, until golden brown. Cool in the pan on a rack for 10 minutes. Remove the cakes from the pan, and let them cool completely. Keep them in an airtight container until the next day.

Berawecka

Dried Fruit and Nut Spiced Loaf

Belonging to the long list of edible gifts traditionally shared in Alsace around Christmas, Berawecka is an enriched bread dough studded with marinated dried fruits, nuts and winter spices. I like to think of it as the French Christmas Pudding, although much, much denser and more wholesome. I love a few thin slices for breakfast topped with butter, or for "apéro" paired with cheese. The list of ingredients is lengthy, but because this festive loaf is so compact and infused with alcohol, it keeps for days and days, and ensures your efforts are well worth it.

SERVES 10 TO 12 / MAKES 2 LOAVES

¼ cup (60 ml) Kirsch

¼ cup (60 ml) water

¼ cup (50 g) sugar

⅓ cup (50 g) black raisins, not packed

⅓ cup (50 g) dried pears, diced, not packed

⅓ cup (50 g) dried black mission figs, diced, not packed

⅓ cup (50 g) dried apricots, diced, not packed

⅓ cup (50 g) dried prunes, diced, not packed

⅓ cup (50 g) dates, diced, not packed

⅓ cup (50 g) candied citrus peels (orange, lemon) diced, not packed

⅓ cup (40 g) chopped walnuts

⅓ cup (50 g) chopped almonds

½ cup (40 g) chopped hazelnuts

2 tsp (5 g) ground cinnamon

1 tsp fresh ground black pepper

1 tsp freshly grated nutmeg

½ tsp aniseed, ground

½ tsp coriander seeds, ground

1 star anise

For the Bread Dough

1 tsp instant yeast

2 cups (250 g) all-purpose flour

½ tsp salt

¼ cup (60 ml) lukewarm water

½ cup (125 ml) milk

2 tbsp (30 g) unsalted butter, melted

The day before baking, in a large bowl, combine the Kirsch, water and sugar. Stir in the raisins, pears, figs, apricots, prunes, dates, citrus peels, walnuts, almonds, hazelnuts, cinnamon, ground pepper, nutmeg, aniseed, coriander seeds and star anise. Cover the bowl with plastic wrap, and let soak overnight in the fridge.

The next day, prepare the bread dough. In a large bowl, combine the instant yeast, all-purpose flour and salt. Stir in the water, milk and butter. Mix until you get a soft, slightly sticky ball of dough. Drain the soaked fruits and nuts, and fold them into the dough in small additions. Divide the dough in two equal parts. Shape each into logs about 2½ x 8½ inches (6 x 22 cm). Wet your hands to smooth out the logs, and place them onto a parchment-lined baking sheet. Cover with a kitchen cloth and let sit for 30 minutes.

Meanwhile, preheat your oven to 390°F (200°C, or gas mark 6), with a rack in the middle.

Bake for 45 minutes, until golden brown. Transfer to a cooling rack, and let cool to room temperature before cutting into thin slices.

Rousquilles

Lemon-Glazed Melt-in-Your-Mouth Cookies

These delightful Catalan ring-shaped cookies have a fragrant sandy crumb encased in a lemony glaze. They are known to be utterly melty and are raved about on both sides of the Franco-Spanish border. Although in Spain, rosquillos are fried and in France they are baked.

The ancestor of rousquilles were little aniseed cookie rings made and sold by street vendors in the Pyrenees Mountains, carried around on wooden sticks. It is said that one day, a local pastry chef had the idea to coat them in a lemon glaze, giving birth to this Catalan classic. Rousquilles can be found in most bakeries in the Pyrenees and are enjoyed all throughout the day—even for apéro, with a glass of local Banyuls wine.

MAKES 18 TO 20 COOKIES

¼ cup plus ½ tbsp (100 g) honey

⅓ cup plus 1 tbsp (73 g) sugar

½ cup (113 g) butter, at room temperature

1 tsp salt

1 lemon, zested

3¼ cups (405 g) all-purpose flour

2 tsp (8 g) baking powder

2 tsp (10 g) aniseed, ground

2 large eggs

For the Lemon Glaze

2½ cups (300 g) powdered sugar

1 lemon, juiced

3–4 tbsp (45–60 ml) water

In a large mixing bowl, cream together the honey, sugar, butter, salt and lemon zest, until fluffy.

In a separate bowl, sift together the all-purpose flour, baking powder and ground aniseed. Combine with the honey mixture, and stir until crumbly in texture.

Add 1 egg and mix until fully incorporated. Add the second egg and mix until the dough comes together into a rough ball.

Place the dough between two sheets of parchment paper and roll it out to a ¾-inch (2-cm) thickness. Chill for 1 hour.

After 1 hour, preheat your oven to 390°F (200°C, or gas mark 6), with a rack in the middle.

Transfer the dough onto a floured work surface, and cut out 18 to 20 circles, 2½ to 3 inches (6 to 8 cm) in diameter. Cut out a ¾-inch (2-cm) hole in the middle of each circle, using a cookie cutter or apple corer. Carefully line up the rings onto a parchment-lined baking sheet.

Cook for 16 to 18 minutes, until slightly golden.

Transfer the cookies immediately onto a cooling rack, and let them cool to room temperature.

To make the lemon glaze, combine the powdered sugar and lemon juice in a small bowl. Slowly start pouring water, 1 tablespoon (15 ml) at a time, mixing continuously and stopping when the glaze is still thick, opaque and just pourable. It should not be too thin or it won't stay on the cookies.

Place a baking sheet underneath the cooling rack. Dip each cookie into the glaze, and gently place them back onto the cooling rack; you can use two forks or chopsticks to do so.

Let set at room temperature for a minimum of 1 hour.

Bugnes Lyonnaises

Lyon-Style Angel Wings

When I was living in Lyon, I remember eyeing these little fried pastries in bakery windows around the city, and I loved how each baker had a twist on them: crunchy or soft, flat or knotted, flavored with citrus or different spices.

They're said to be an import from the city of Rome, where they were prepared for carnivals. They have become a specialty in Lyon, Saint-Étienne and the entire Savoy region. They are traditionally enjoyed for Mardi-Gras, in February, and even year-round—slightly disrespecting the tradition of Lent.

They are fun to make and can be a great baking project with kids, who will devour them afterwards. They are pillowy inside but have a nice crunch too—the perfect mix! I like to flavor them with vanilla and lemon zest, but you can try them with bergamot or orange zest, ginger, cardamom or even saffron.

SERVES 8 / MAKES 16 TO 18 BUGNES

2⅓ cups (290 g) all-purpose flour

3 tbsp (38 g) sugar

1½ tsp (6 g) baking powder

½ tsp salt

⅓ cup plus 1 tbsp (100 g) unsalted butter, at room temperature

3 large eggs

1 tsp vanilla extract

1 lemon, zested

Vegetable oil, for frying

Powdered sugar, for topping

In a large mixing bowl, combine the all-purpose flour, sugar, baking powder and salt. Cut the butter into small cubes and mix it into the dry ingredients with your fingers. Add in the eggs, one by one, mixing well between each addition. The dough will become easier to work with and smoother after the addition of each egg. Add in the vanilla extract and lemon zest, and shape the dough into a ball. Cover the bowl with a kitchen towel, and refrigerate for 3 hours.

Divide the dough into four equal parts. On a floured work surface, roll the first piece of dough into a ⅛-inch (4-mm)-thick rectangle. Using a pastry wheel or a sharp knife, cut the rectangle into 2-inch (5-cm) rhombus/diamond shapes. With a sharp knife, make a 1-inch (2.5-cm) slit lengthwise in the middle of each diamond, grab a corner, pass it through the slit and pull lightly to create a twist. Repeat with the other three pieces of dough. Lay the bugnes under a kitchen cloth as you go. Line a large plate with paper towels.

Heat vegetable oil in a heavy pan over medium heat and fry the bugnes in batches of about 5—not more, or they won't cook properly—for about 3 to 4 minutes on each side until puffed and golden.

Transfer the bugnes to a paper towel–lined plate, and continue to fry the remainder in batches.

Serve immediately, topped with powdered sugar.

Teurgoule

Slow-Baked Cinnamon Rice Pudding

Normandy sure knows the art of comfort food, and this old-fashioned rice pudding is no exception.

The quirky name Teurgoule means "twisted mouth," supposedly because of the faces locals would make when tasting this dish for the first time . . . not out of disgust, but astonishment, as cinnamon was such a foreign-tasting spice. In fact, in the eighteenth century, as ships from the Indias imported rum and vanilla to the city of Nantes, giving birth to the Gâteau Nantais (page 110), they imported rice and cinnamon to the Honfleur port, in Lower Normandy, giving birth to this cinnamon-spiced rice pudding, made with local milk from Normandy cows.

Unlike most rice puddings, this one is baked for several hours in the oven to create an utterly creamy pudding topped with a thick caramelized skin. In Normandy, it is traditionally enjoyed with a slice of brioche called fallue and a glass of dry cider.

SERVES 6 / MAKES 1 TEURGOULE

4¼ cups (1 L) milk (2% or whole)

½ cup (100 g) sugar

1 tsp ground cinnamon

⅓ cup (65 g) arborio rice

½ tsp salt

Preheat your oven to 300°F (150°C, or gas mark 2), with a rack in the middle.

In a medium saucepan, combine the milk, sugar and cinnamon. Bring to a simmer, and take the pan off the stove immediately.

Combine the rice and salt in a deep earthenware dish, and pour the sweet milk on top.

Bake for 3½ hours, until a thick brown skin has formed on top.

Take out of the oven and enjoy warm.

Canistrelli au Citron et à l'Anis

White Wine, Lemon and Aniseed Cookies

Like the Prune Flan (page 148) to the Bretons, or the Kugelhopf (page 141) to the Alsatians, canistrelli are little bites of childhood for most Corsican people. These crunchy cookies made from white wine bread loaves, cut cross-ways and twice baked, are beloved all throughout the island. They're reminiscent of Italian biscotti, although they are slightly crumblier—and just a bit better if you ask me.

Their creation is very easy and calls for only a few ingredients that you already likely have in your pantry. With oil and white wine replacing any sort of dairy or eggs, these are also naturally vegan. The traditional version is subtly flavored with lemon zest and aniseeds, but you can customize these as you prefer by adding nuts, dried fruits or chocolate.

In Corsica, canistrelli are often eaten dunked in wine, but they are just as perfect with a warm cup of coffee or tea.

MAKES 28 TO 32 CANISTRELLI

3 cups plus 2 tbsp (400 g) all-purpose flour

2 tsp (8 g) baking powder

1 tsp salt

¾ cup plus 1½ tbsp (170 g) sugar

2 lemons, zested

4 tsp (20 g) aniseed, whole

⅔ cup (160 ml) neutral-flavored oil (i.e., rapeseed)

½ cup (125 ml) dry white wine

4 tbsp (50 g) sugar, for topping

Preheat your oven to 335°F (170°C, or gas mark 3), with a rack in the middle.

In a large mixing bowl, combine the all-purpose flour, baking powder, salt, sugar, lemon zest and aniseed. Add the oil and white wine, and stir until the dough comes together into a rough ball.

Divide the dough in two, and shape the two pieces into two 10- to 12-inch (25- to 31-cm)-long logs. Roll each log in 1 tablespoon (13 g) of sugar to coat it all around. Carefully transfer the two logs onto a parchment-lined baking sheet.

Bake the logs for 30 minutes. Take them out of the oven—leave the oven on—and let the logs cool down for 15 minutes on the baking sheet. Slice the logs into ½-inch (1.3-cm) slices and lay them flat on the baking sheet, cut-side down, and bake for an additional 20 minutes, flipping the slices after 10 minutes.

Transfer the canistrelli to a cooling rack to cool to room temperature.

Acknowledgments

Thank you to Marc. My recipe tester, proofreader, photo endorser, dish cleaner, spirit lifter and best life partner.

Thank you to my parents for always keeping their doors open when I'm in France, and for always having made, and always keeping, France my home.

Thank you to my publisher Page Street Publishing and my editor, Rebecca Fofonoff, for believing in me and in my vision, and for offering me the wonderful opportunity to write this book. Rebecca, your support, insight and recommendations were valuable in so many ways.

I would also like to thank the rest of the team at Page Street Publishing, especially Rosie Stewart and Meg Baskis.

Thank you to Jenna Nelson Patton for her passion and professionalism during the copyediting phase.

Thank you to Karly Schaefer, for complementing this book with her lovely lifestyle photographs.

Thank you to Anna DiMaurizia for the use of her beautiful kitchen.

Last, but certainly not least, thank you to my all blog readers and followers for tagging along on my food journeys, and for sharing my passion for France and French food.

About the Author

Audrey is the creator of the successful blog *Pardon Your French*, where she shares recipes and stories from her beloved country, France. She was born and raised in Brittany, on the Atlantic coast of France, where she naturally developed a taste for good food and visual storytelling. Audrey lived and studied in several parts of France, Finland and Australia before settling in Niagara, Canada, ten years ago with her husband. After obtaining her master of communications and foreign languages, she began a full-time career in marketing. Audrey started her blog to share her lifelong passion for French homecooking with others and to document French recipes and French-food focused stories. Audrey is a self-taught cook and photographer, and has established herself as a French food authority in Canada and in the United States, working as a photographer, recipe developer, food writer and consultant for companies in the food and drink industry.

Index